a kitchen year

Paula McIntyre

Gill & Macmillan

Gill & Macmillan Ltd
Hume Avenue
Park West
Dublin 12
with associated companies throughout the world
www.gillmacmillan.ie

© Paula McIntyre 2008

978 07171 4321 4

Photographs by Hugh McElveen
Index compiled by Cover to Cover
Book design and typesetting by Design Image
Printed by Oriental Press, Dubai

3 5 4 2

For my parents, Davy and Rae, and grandparents, Jim and Kathleen

a kitchen year

contents

acknowledgments

Thanks to everyone at Gill & Macmillan, especially Emma Farrell, Sarah Liddy, Kristin Jensen and Marshall Matchett for the massive support in producing the book.

To everyone at BBC Northern Ireland, but in particular Susan Lovell, Peter Johnson, Maggie Doyle, Jackie Neill, Pauline Currie, Noel Russell, Claire Burgoyne, John Toal, Roisin Brown, Regina Gallen, Clare Delargy, Olivia Higgins, Michael Higgins and all in Studio 8.

Thanks to Paul and Joyce Carroll for kindly lending me their wonderful facilities at Ghan House in Carlingford, Co. Louth for the photographs in the book.

To Hugh McElveen for the fantastic photographs and to Sarah Liddy for her brilliant input into the photo shoot.

To Equinox in Belfast for the use of some of the crockery and glasses.

To Jane McAuley for the use of extra crockery and for pulling me out of many diffs over the years!

To my colleagues at Northern Regional College Ballymoney and Newtownabbey campuses.

Thanks to Jim Flanagan, editor of *Sunday Life*, to Colette Flanagan, to *Sunday Life* features editor Audrey Watson, Mark McCormick and photographer Ian Magill.

Thanks to Raymond and Nicola Reihill and family. Thanks also to Anne Marie McAleese.

To Judith Gilder and Chris Pickering for their invaluable support in Manchester.

Thanks to my brother David and sister-in-law Dorothy for the love, support and problem solving, and to Andrew and Rachel for being the best nephew and niece anyone could ask for.

To my grandparents Jim and Kathleen.

And finally, to my parents Davy and Rae for unending love, support and understanding.

introduction

My first kitchen memory is of standing on a stool to reach the worktop, wearing a red apron and making tealoaf with my mother. I was about five years old at the time and will never forget the magical transformation of grey, sludgey batter into gorgeous, golden cake. It was intoxicating and I haven't really stopped cooking since.

When I left school, I went to college in Belfast to study hotel management but did all my placements in the kitchen of the Ramore Restaurant in Portrush. The food here was fabulous and cutting edge for Ireland at the time, and the chef, George McAlpin, was a patient, understanding and thoroughly lovely man. Unfortunately, this was not a realistic introduction to the catering industry and I got a very rude awakening when I moved to London to work in testosterone-fuelled and slightly violent kitchens. It was a relief when I got news that I'd won a scholarship to an American university, Johnson and Wales in Rhode Island, for three months on an international exchange. What I didn't realise was that this would change my whole relationship with food. In 1989, America was light years ahead of Europe in terms of culinary innovation. I stayed on at the university for another year and a half as a teaching assistant in culinary arts, soaking up the influences around me like a sponge.

Most chefs want to have their own restaurant and I was keen to give it a go. Full of youthful, naive enthusiasm, I was all fired up and ready for action! The chance of a business in Manchester seemed liked the perfect solution. I spent five years cooking what I wanted to and honing the style I have today.

I returned to Ireland in 1997. It was at this time I met a producer from BBC Radio Ulster and began to contribute to various shows on Radio Ulster. I appeared on *Ready, Steady, Cook* a couple of times and had my own television show, *Taste for*

Adventure, on BBC2 Northern Ireland. In 2001, my radio show *McIntyre Magic* had the first of three series. I now present the cooking slot on the *Saturday Magazine* with John Toal.

I adore the combination of broadcasting and cooking, but my real goal has always been to publish a cookbook. Over the years, I've half-heartedly toyed with having a go at writing, but two things gave me the kick up the behind that I needed. First, the *Sunday Life* newspaper gave me my own weekly cooking column, which has taught me the discipline of deadlines. Also, at the time, BBC Radio Ulster producer Clare Burgoyne was in charge of the *Saturday Magazine*. Buoyed up by people ringing the show to ask if I had a book out, she encouraged me do a synopsis and get a few photos taken. Serendipitously, Marshall Matchett from Gill & Macmillan rang at the same time, and after a few meetings, the book was commissioned.

Putting together the recipes for this book has been one of the most enjoyable times of my life. My summer holidays from college were spent cooking the recipes and having dinner for friends in the evenings. I then had the brilliant task of going to Ghan House in Carlingford, Co. Louth for a week to have the photos taken for the book.

Seasonal cooking is very much a passion of mine. I abhor strawberries and asparagus at Christmas and parsnips in midsummer. Eating seasonally makes sense for flavour, economics and quality. I am also fiercely proud of the fantastic produce we have in Ireland – our meat, fish, vegetables, cheese, artisan producers and dairy are the best in the world. This book combines seasonal food, local produce and a bit of a twist with some exotic ingredients as well. The recipes are very much what you need to eat at different times of the year, hence the Latin feel to January, the barbecue in August and comfort food in the autumn months.

This is very much a home cookbook. Although I trained as a chef, this is not a po-faced, serious cheffy book. It's the food I serve either for simple suppers or for having friends around. I don't want to use the term 'dinner party' because it brings me back to the 1990s, when you had to have a tortured, oversculpted starter, an elaborate main course and a choice of at least four desserts. The best parties I go to are where a big pot is plopped in the middle of the table and everyone digs in. Cooking for friends and family is an act of love that you should relish and have fun with. Keep things simple.

I want you to use this book, to have sauce spilled on the pages and for the book to open naturally at the recipes you use the most. I hope you enjoy reading and using the book as much as I have loved the experience of putting it together.

a kitchen year

january

january

January has all the potential to be a sullen, depressing month. Over Christmas, you've given your credit card a real battering, eaten too much rich food and then all you hear is the diet police bleating on about 'new year, new you, eating lifestyles that will change your life'.

Leeks are in full swing at this time of year. Gorgeous on their own, steamed and finished with a simple mustard vinaigrette or baked with a sharp cheddar sauce, they are also a vital part of winter soups. Boil a ham hock with aromatic vegetables to use as the base for stock and then shred the meat from the ham to give heart to the finished soup. Ham and leeks are a well-known match and are fantastic in a soup. And you can't have soup without bread, so I've included one of my favourites – potato and smoked cheddar rolls, which have a spongy texture and are addictive when they first come out of the oven.

Latin American cooking will always gladden the heart – can you really visualise anyone sitting depressed in January in Rio? The weather may be better, but I think the cooking may have something to do with it too. I mail order dried chipotle, guajillo, ancho and poblano chillies – the thrill of receiving the package and its sexy, sultry contents is enough to brighten any dull day. And the taste! Chillies run the gamut of tastes in the same way as wines, and the terminology used – hints of tobacco, leather, smoky, citrus – could describe a poblano chilli or a Bordeaux wine. Combine these gems with spices like cumin and coriander to create robust, feisty dishes that kick any seasonal culinary disorders in to touch.

And even though the diet police would hate it, a month without chocolate would be criminal. Rich hot chocolate sponge, saturated with caramelised nuts, served with dulce de leche and candied pecan ice. January blues? You've got to be kidding!

leek, ham hock and cannellini bean soup

Serves 4

The list of ingredients for this soup is like a veritable seasonal comfort food feast – leeks, ham, onions, garlic, beans, potatoes and carrots. This is my favourite kind of soup – home-made stock, puréed with the vegetables it was boiled with (no waste), then combined with chunky ham, whole beans and chunky leeks. When making any soup, the stock is vital. Boiling ham on the bone will give loads of flavour anyway, but add aromatic vegetables like carrots, celery, onion and parsley stalks and your kitchen will smell like heaven. Leeks in January will have had the benefits of frost, which is vital for winter vegetables. Use every part of the leek – throwing out the pungent green leaves should be a criminal offence!

2 ham hocks
2 onions
2 medium carrots, peeled and cut into 3 cm-
  thick chunks
2 stalks celery, cut into 3 cm-thick chunks
2 sprigs fresh thyme
4 cloves garlic
handful fresh parsley
2 medium potatoes
olive oil
1 large leek, split, washed and chopped
250 g dried cannellini beans, soaked overnight
  then boiled until soft
salt and pepper

Wash the ham hocks and place in a large saucepan. Cover with cold water. Peel and quarter one of the onions and add to the ham hocks with the carrots, celery, thyme and garlic. Pick the leaves from the parsley and set aside and add the stalks to the ham hocks. Bring to the boil and simmer for 1 hour.

Peel and cut the potatoes into chunks and add to the pot. Continue to cook for 45 minutes. Remove the ham from the pot and set aside. Purée the rest of the mixture in a food processor and strain through a sieve. Rip all the meat from the ham hock and chop roughly.

Heat a pan with 2 tablespoons of oil and add the remaining onion, chopped finely, and the chopped leek. Cook with a lid on, on a low heat for 5 minutes. Add the purée, cooked beans and ham and simmer for 10 minutes. Add the chopped parsley leaves, check the seasoning and serve.

potato, onion and smoked cheddar bread

Makes 2 loaves

Using potatoes in a yeast bread might seem strange, but it works brilliantly in traditional potato bread, so why not? In this recipe, you use mashed potatoes plus the water they're cooked in, which produces a spongy textured soft bread. Onions cooked slowly in olive oil until soft, golden and sticky are a joy to eat. Combine them with a soft bread and smoked cheese, and they're positively ethereal!

500 g peeled potatoes
200 g chopped butter
1 teaspoon salt
1 tablespoon caster sugar
1 onion, finely chopped
100 g grated smoked cheddar
2 x 7 g sachets yeast
1 kg strong flour
2 tablespoons olive oil
1 egg yolk, beaten

Boil the potatoes until soft. Drain 500 ml of the hot cooking liquid into a measuring jug and then place in a large mixing bowl. Squeeze the cooked potatoes through a sieve on top of the cooking liquid. Add the butter, salt and sugar and leave to melt. Leave to cool.

Cook the onion in the oil until golden and add to the potato mixture. When cool, add the cheese and yeast and start to mix in the flour (you could do this in a food processor with a dough hook). Turn the dough onto a floured board and knead – massage with the heel of your hands, stretching the dough and then folding it back. Do this until you feel resistance from the dough. Brush a bowl with a little oil and place the dough in the bowl, covering with a warm, damp tea towel. Leave for 1 hour.

Knock the dough with your fist and knead for 30 seconds. Divide into two pieces and roll into a round loaf shape. Brush with the beaten egg yolk and dust round the edges with a little flour. Place on a floured baking sheet and preheat the oven to 200°C.

When the oven is hot, cook the dough for 30 minutes or until the bottom of the loaf sounds hollow when you tap it. Cool on wire racks.

chorizo and potato empanadas

Serves 4

Empanadas are Spanish pastries filled with whatever takes your fancy – cheese, vegetables, meat or fish. In this case, I'm using chorizo, potatoes and spices – comfort food with a splash of passion! Just think Antonio Banderas with a pair of slippers. Empanadas are great on their own, but the accompanying mojo dressing (a fulfilling dressing from Latin cuisine; see p. 8) will lift them to new levels.

Empanada dough:
400 g plain flour
100 g polenta
1 teaspoon salt
4 tablespoons olive oil
50 g melted butter
1 egg
1 egg yolk
200 ml cold water

Filling:
1 tablespoon olive oil
100 g chorizo, chopped into ½ cm pieces
1 medium red onion, finely chopped
2 cloves garlic, crushed
1 teaspoon ground cumin
1 teaspoon sweet smoked paprika
250 g baby potatoes, boiled in salted water,
  peeled and cut into 1 cm dice
salt and pepper
handful of fresh chopped coriander
2 egg yolks

To make the dough, sift the flour into a bowl, then add the polenta and salt. Mix well, then make a well in the centre. Add the oil, butter, egg and egg yolk. Mix with the water to make a soft dough. Wrap in cling film and chill for 30 minutes.

To make the filling, heat the oil in a large frying pan over a high heat and add the chorizo (its oil will be released). Lower the heat and add the onion and garlic and cook until soft. Add the ground cumin and paprika and cook for 1 minute, then fold in the potatoes. Season with salt and pepper and add the coriander. Set aside the mixture to cool.

Divide the dough into 12 equal-sized pieces. Roll each piece into a ball and then roll on a lightly floured surface to ¼ cm thick. Brush round the edges with the egg yolk and place a round of the filling in the middle. Fold over into a half moon shape and seal the edges. Place on a lightly floured baking sheet. Repeat with the remaining dough. You could make smaller sized ones for nibbles.

Preheat the oven to 180°C. Bake the empanadas for 20 minutes or until golden brown. Serve immediately with the roast garlic, red onion and chilli mojo on the next page.

roast garlic, red onion and chilli mojo

A mojo is a thick Latin American dressing, not as runny as a vinaigrette and not as chunky as a salsa, making it ideal for dipping. This is great with the empanadas but would work well with roast baby potatoes or chips as well. Roasting garlic gives it a candied sweetness that dispels its harsh 'rawness' in dressings.

1 bulb garlic
vegetable oil
1 large red chilli
1 medium red onion, chopped
juice of 1 lime
100 ml extra virgin olive oil or avocado oil
½ teaspoon caster sugar
salt and pepper
handful of fresh chopped coriander

Preheat the oven to 200°C.

Break the garlic into cloves but don't remove the skin. Place in an ovenproof ramekin and pour over the vegetable oil to submerge the garlic. Cover with tin foil and bake for 20 minutes.

Lightly brush the chilli with oil and roast in the oven for 10 minutes or until the skin is scorched. Cool the chilli and peel, deseed, and chop it. Cool the garlic and pop out of its skin. Use 2 cloves for this dressing and place the rest in a jam jar, cover with oil and keep for up to 2 weeks in the fridge (the garlic is great smeared over toasted ciabatta and the oil can be used in dressings).

Crush the 2 cooked garlic cloves and mix in a bowl with the chopped roasted chilli, onion, lime juice, oil and sugar. Season well and add the chopped coriander.

fried oyster tacos with coriander crema and fennel slaw

Serves 4

If you've never tried oysters, first try eating them cooked before going down the traditional raw route. Fried fish in a taco (not the corn shells available commercially), wrapped in a fresh flour tortilla with sauce and crunchy leaves, is a heaven-sent way of enjoying them. Purists may be appalled, but oysters lend themselves to being lightly coated and fried and zingy flavours pep them up brilliantly. By all means, buy ready-made tortillas, but the difference between them and the ones straight off the griddle is huge. It might be a bit of effort, but if you compare the smell, texture and look of fresh-baked bread to a pan loaf, you can taste the difference.

Soft flour tortillas:
400 g plain flour
75 g chopped butter
1 teaspoon salt
150 ml water

Coriander crema:
100 ml sour cream
1 tablespoon mayonnaise
zest of 1 lime
handful of fresh coriander, chopped
salt and pepper, to taste

Fennel slaw:
1 large red chilli pepper
4 tablespoons olive oil
juice and zest of 1 lime
1 teaspoon caster sugar
1 bulb fennel
1 red onion
1 red pepper
4 tablespoons good-quality mayonnaise
salt and pepper

Fried oysters:
24 opened oysters (ask your fishmonger but
   use them within 6 hours)
150 g polenta
25 g finely grated Parmesan
100 g plain flour
½ teaspoon chilli powder
salt and pepper
2 eggs
50 ml milk
oil for cooking

To make the tortillas, rub the flour and butter together to a mixture that resembles fine breadcrumbs. Add the salt and water to bind into a dough. Wrap in cling film and chill for 20 minutes.

Divide the dough into 12 equal sized pieces. Roll each piece into a ball and then roll out as thinly as you can. Place an appropriately sized plate on top of the rolled dough and cut around it to tidy it up.

Heat a frying pan or griddle pan over medium-high heat and place the tortilla in the pan. When bubbles appear on the surface, flip over and cook for another minute on the other side. Repeat with the remaining dough and separate each cooked tortilla in between greaseproof paper.

To make the coriander crema, mix all the ingredients together and check the seasoning. Set aside.

To make the fennel slaw, brush the chilli with a little of the oil and roast in a 200°C oven until the skin is blistered and going dark. Place in a plastic bag for 5 minutes. Peel the chilli, remove the seeds and chop finely.

Place the lime juice in a bowl with the sugar. Cut the fennel into quarters, through the root. Remove the root at the bottom and shred the fennel as finely as possible (if you're brave, use a mandoline). Toss the fennel with the lime juice and sugar and add the remaining olive oil. Season with salt.

Peel the onion, cut in half and slice as thinly as you can. Top and tail the pepper and slice the flesh away from the seeds. Shred as thinly as you can, slicing the top and tail as well. Mix this into the fennel mix with the onion, roasted chilli and mayonnaise. Check for seasoning and set aside.

To make the fried oysters, rinse and drain the oysters. Mix the polenta and cheese together. Season the flour in a separate bowl with the chilli powder, salt and pepper. Whisk the eggs and milk together and put into a third separate bowl. Dip each oyster into the flour and shake off the excess, then dip into the egg mixture and then into the polenta. Repeat with all the oysters.

Heat half a thumbnail depth of oil in a frying pan over medium heat and cook the oysters (don't overcrowd the pan) until golden and crisp. Drain on kitchen paper.

To assemble the taco, take a tortilla and spread with the coriander crema, sprinkle over the fennel slaw and then run 4 oysters up the middle. Roll and eat immediately. Repeat with the remaining tortillas. It's a good idea to get your guests to make these themselves – just put everything in the middle of the table.

pork mole

Serves 4

Mole, literally translated, means 'a mixture'. Mole negro, meaning 'black mixture', has the addition of chocolate, which is the type most people are familiar with. I prefer a rich red mole, and while this is not a traditional recipe, it combines the kick of chillies, the creaminess of nuts and the heat of spices. You can use fresh chillies to good effect, but it's worth seeking out good-quality dried varieties from Mexico. My favourite combination for this is a mixture of chipotle (smoked jalapeños) and guajillo (fruity and not too hot). Dried chillies have an intense complexity of flavour that the fresh ones don't really have. Combine all the ingredients in a food processor, pour over sealed pork, and cook – simple, yet stunningly uplifting. You could use chicken stock cubes in this recipe, but home-made, while a bit of effort, is infinitely better. Make up a good batch and freeze what you don't need to use for soups and other sauces.

Small pieces of pork work well for this and I find the cheaper the cut, the longer the cooking and the better the flavour. Ask your butcher for shoulder pieces.

Serve this dish with quinoa and beans (p. 13). Or you could serve this simply with some boiled rice or a stack of the tortillas from the recipe on p. 9, but there's something about the combination of hot chilli, spices and tasty pork with sweet potatoes that gets my juices flowing every time.

Rich chicken stock:
1 kg chicken wings
1 carrot, peeled and roughly chopped
1 leek, split, washed and chopped
2 onions, peeled and roughly chopped
2 stalks celery, chopped
a few sprigs fresh thyme

Pork mole:
1 kg pork fillet
6 ripe tomatoes
1 guajillo chilli
2 chipotle chillies
1 onion, peeled and roughly chopped
4 cloves garlic
2 teaspoons toasted, ground cumin seeds
75 g toasted pistachios or almonds
salt and pepper
olive oil for cooking
500 ml chicken stock

To make the chicken stock, preheat the oven to 200°C. Place all the ingredients, apart from the thyme, in a roasting tray and cook until golden brown, about 30 minutes. Transfer everything to a large pot, leaving any fat behind. Add the fresh thyme. Cover well with cold water, bring to the boil and simmer for 4 hours (cover with more water if it evaporates). Strain and cool. Pour what you don't need into freezer bags.

pork mole

smoky quinoa and beans

To make the mole, trim the pork fillet and cut into 2 cm-thick medallions. Blend the tomatoes, chillies, onion, garlic, cumin and nuts in a food processor to a thick paste. Season the pork with salt and pepper.

Heat 1 tablespoon of oil in a frying pan and heat until smoking. Add half the pork, sealing for 2 minutes on each side. Place the pork in a casserole dish and repeat with the remaining pork. Add the mole paste to the pan, cook for 1 minute and add the stock. Warm through and then add to the pork. Place a lid on the casserole and simmer for 1 hour.

This dish can be made successfully with cheaper cuts of pork, like shoulder or loin – just increase the cooking time if necessary.

Quinoa is a Latin American seed that puffs up like couscous. It's ideal for coeliacs and is packed with protein. It soaks up other ingredients wonderfully and is fantastic with the mole.

2 tablespoons olive oil
1 red onion, finely chopped
2 cloves garlic, crushed
1 teaspoon sweet smoked paprika
400 ml stock (vegetable or chicken, made from
  1 cube)
200 g quinoa
1 x 400 g tin pinto beans, drained
handful fresh chopped coriander
salt and pepper

Heat the oil in a saucepan over medium heat and add the onion and garlic. Cook until the onions are soft, about 5 minutes, then add the smoked paprika. Cook for a further 1 minute, then add the stock. Bring to the boil and add the quinoa. Turn the heat down to a simmer, cover the quinoa with a lid and cook for 15 minutes. Turn off the heat, leave the lid on and leave the quinoa to puff up for a further 15 minutes. Remove the lid, add the beans and coriander and check the seasoning.

caramel, chocolate and Brazil nut cake

Serves 4

I first made this cake on the BBC's *Saturday Magazine* radio programme for Fairtrade Fortnight. The point was to pack as many Fairtrade products into one dish as possible. Serendipitously, the Fairtrade Brazil nuts worked a treat with the chocolate. This is a delicious cake on its own, but turn it upside down to let the nutty, caramel topping sink in and you have something wonderful.

Caramel topping:
75 g melted butter
75 g light brown sugar
2 dessertspoons honey
75 g chopped Brazil nuts

Cake batter:
100 g softened butter
150 g soft brown sugar
3 large eggs, lightly whisked with a fork
175 g self-raising flour
1 level teaspoon baking soda
50 g good-quality cocoa
150 ml buttermilk

To make the topping, generously butter a 10-inch spring form cake tin and add the remaining butter to the bottom of the tin. Sprinkle the sugar over the butter. Dip a spoon into boiling water and then into the honey and drizzle this over the sugar and butter mixture. Finally, sprinkle over the nuts and preheat the oven to 180°C.

To make the cake, beat the butter and sugar with a whisk until pale and fluffy. Add the beaten eggs in a steady stream, beating all the time. Sift the flour, baking soda and cocoa into a bowl and add to the butter mixture in three batches, adding a third of the buttermilk each time. Whisk to a smooth batter and pour on top of the nut mixture. Bake for 35 minutes or until an inserted skewer comes out clean. Remove the cake from the oven and turn upside down onto a plate, but don't remove the tin. Leave for 5 minutes to allow the caramel to soak in and then remove the tin. This is best served warm either with cream, ice cream or the dulce de leche and candied pecan semifreddo on p. 15.

dulce de leche and candied pecan semifreddo

Serves 4

Dulce de leche is a fancy Spanish way of talking about banoffee toffee. It's now widely available in this country and saves boiling condensed milk in a submerged pan of boiling water for 2 hours. Many households have horror stories about peeling the contents of an exploded condensed milk tin from the kitchen ceiling, so this ready-made delight couldn't have come soon enough. This iced dessert is a sublime accompaniment to the caramel, chocolate and Brazil nut cake on p. 14, but is also great in the summer with honey-roasted peaches.

Dulce de leche mixture:
3 large egg yolks
50 g caster sugar
350 ml double cream
100 g dulce de leche
splash of golden rum (optional)

Candied pecans:
75 g caster sugar
1 tablespoon water
100 g pecan nuts

To make the dulce de leche mixture, whisk the egg yolks and sugar in a glass or metal bowl over a saucepan of hot water, making sure the bottom of the bowl and the hot water aren't touching. Whisk until pale and creamy and the actual whisk leaves a track when dragged through the mix. Remove from the heat.

Place 100 ml of the cream and the dulce de leche in a saucepan and warm through. Whisk this into the egg mixture. Cool.

Lightly whip the remaining cream to soft peaks and then fold into the dulce de leche mixture. Fold in a splash of rum.

To make the candied pecans, boil the sugar and water in a heavy-based saucepan. Don't stir this mixture, as the sugar will crystallise – merely swirl it around the pan. When the mix is amber coloured, add the nuts, mix around and pour onto non-stick parchment paper to cool.

When hard and cool, chop the pecans and fold into the dulce de leche mixture. Pour into a plastic container or loaf tin lined with cling film and freeze for at least 4 hours.

To serve, remove the semifreddo from the freezer 10 minutes before serving. Turn upside down and pull from the tin with the cling film. Place a knife under a hot tap or dip into a jug of hot water and slice.

a kitchen year

february

february

This is a month absolutely chock full of celebrations – Pancake Tuesday, Valentine's Day and my personal favourite: the short, forced rhubarb season.

To warm things up, there's creamy onion soup and a traditional Irish potato bread recipe with a Native American twist.

Mardi Gras, literally 'fat Tuesday', or Pancake Tuesday, is one of my favourite days. I adore pancakes and a guilt-free excuse to eat as many as possible gets my vote every time. I've included a savoury pancake in the form of a scallion crêpe filled with five-spiced duck and also a sweet griddle-style pancake. When I was young, my mother used to make pancakes every Saturday morning – they never really reached the table, as my brother and I would snatch them the second they were ready, smearing them thickly with butter and jam. I've given the pancakes here a grown-up feel with a ginger injection, rum and raisin compote and cinnamon mascarpone.

If you're in a relationship, ignore Valentine's Day at your peril, and if you're not, cook the dinner for friends you love anyway – crispy prawns, rib-eye steaks, roast baby beetroot, red wine butter and stuffed baby potatoes (trust me, stuffing baby potatoes for more than two portions will prove a friendship beyond anything!).

As far as local produce goes, February can be a lacklustre month – apples, spuds, a few sprouts and leeks and that's about it. And then forced rhubarb comes along in all its delicate, lovely pink gorgeousness and makes this month something to really look forward to. To go along with the romantic feel to the Valentine's dinner, I've made the rhubarb into a delicate compote with fragrant lemongrass combined with a creamy but cool cream cheese sorbet and crunchy orange praline crumbs.

creamy onion soup with garlic and chives

Serves 4

Golden roasted onions blended into a creamy soup on a cold February day – need I say more?

4 large white onions
2 tablespoons olive oil
salt and pepper
sprigs of fresh thyme and rosemary
25 g butter
1 tablespoon olive oil
2 sticks celery, roughly chopped
4 cloves garlic, chopped
1½ litres chicken stock (see p. 11)
1 medium potato, peeled and chopped
100 ml crème fraîche
bunch chives, chopped

Preheat the oven to 200°C.

Cut the onions in half through the root, with the skin on, and place in a baking dish, flesh side up. Drizzle over the 2 tablespoons of oil and season with salt and pepper. Scatter over the thyme and rosemary. Cover with foil and bake until golden and soft, about 45 minutes.

Heat the butter and 1 tablespoon of oil in a large saucepan over medium heat. Add the celery and place a lid on top. Cook for 5 minutes, stirring occasionally to stop the celery from catching. Remove the lid and add the garlic and cook until golden. Add the stock, bring to the boil and then simmer with the potato until the potato is soft, about 20 minutes. Scoop the onion out of its skin into the pan and simmer for a further 5 minutes. Blend in a liquidiser to a smooth purée and then pass through a sieve into another pan. Heat gently and then stir in the crème fraîche. Season well with salt and pepper. Pour into warmed bowls and garnish with the chives.

sparbled fadge

Serves 4

Fadge is potato bread. Sparbled literally means 'mixed together'. My mother's late lifelong friend, Jean Wilkin, gave me this idea – she was an accomplished traditional cook and a fount of knowledge on old recipes. It's different from traditional potato bread in that it has a little maize meal (polenta) added to the mix. This might not sound traditionally Irish, but in fact, using the maize meal originates from the time that it was sent to Ireland from the United States during the Famine. It's also called Indian meal (as in Native American Indian).

500 g cooked floury potatoes
100 g maize meal
100 g plain flour
pinch sugar
½ teaspoon salt
oil for frying

Drain the potatoes well, then return to the saucepan over a low heat with the lid on. Give them a little shake – do this for a minute to completely dry the potatoes. If you have a potato ricer, pass the potatoes through it into a bowl while warm. Alternatively, mash the potatoes, getting rid of any lumps.

Add the maize meal, flour, sugar and salt and mix to a smooth dough. Turn onto a floured surface and knead together for a minute. Roll into a ball and roll out into a 15 cm circle. Cut around the dough with a plate for an even size. Cut into 8 wedges. Dip a piece of kitchen paper into oil and smear it around a frying pan or griddle pan. Heat over a medium heat and add the fadge. Cook the fadge for 5 to 8 minutes on each side, or until golden brown. Either serve immediately with butter or cool and fry in bacon fat or butter.

ginger prawn lettuce cups with chilli and lime

Serves 2

Even if you're a diehard cynic, you've got to agree that Valentine's Day is a welcome excuse for a bit of post-Christmas decadence. And like Christmas, you'll regret being a killjoy if you choose to ignore it. The Valentine's menu here is great to treat a loved one, or just cook it to celebrate the lovely produce available now – prawns, beef fillet, beetroot and forced rhubarb (p. 31).

100 g rice flour
good pinch salt
150 ml cold sparkling ginger ale
1 teaspoon finely grated root ginger
1 egg white
½ teaspoon sesame oil
2 little gem lettuces
½ cucumber
zest and juice of 1 lime
1 teaspoon chopped, deseeded red chilli
2 tablespoons mayonnaise
2 tablespoons olive or avocado oil
salt and pepper
oil for cooking
12 raw, peeled tiger prawns

Sift the rice flour and salt into a bowl and make a well in the centre. Pour in the ginger ale and grated root ginger and add the egg white and sesame oil. Whisk to a smooth batter. Set aside for 10 minutes.

Break apart the lettuce leaves and place 6 large ones on a platter or large plate. Peel the cucumber, cut it in half lengthways and scoop out the seeds with a teaspoon. Cut into lengths and then dice. Mix this with the lime zest and juice, chilli, mayonnaise and olive oil. Season to taste. Spoon this mixture into the lettuce cups.

Heat a thumbnail's depth of oil in a frying pan or wok over a medium heat. To check if it's ready, add a drop of the batter – if it sizzles, it's ready. Dip each prawn into the batter and then in the oil. Cook for 3 minutes, or until golden. Drain on kitchen paper and serve immediately on top of the lettuce cups.

rib-eye steaks with pancetta, Taleggio and roast garlic

Serves 2

Beef rib-eye is my favourite cut of steak – so much more flavour than fillet or sirloin and a lot cheaper too. Studding it with garlic and herbs and wrapping it in smoked pancetta gives the whole thing a great flavour injection. Roasting garlic brings out its natural sweetness and takes the harshness away from garlic dressings. Keep in the fridge covered in its own oil for up to a month.

Serve this with the roast baby beetroot and stuffed potatoes on p. 25 and the red wine butter on p. 26.

Roast garlic:
2 bulbs garlic
100 ml olive oil
sprigs of fresh thyme and rosemary

Rib-eyes:
2 x centre cut, 250 g rib-eye steaks
1 teaspoon chopped fresh thyme
1 teaspoon chopped fresh rosemary
6 rashers smoked pancetta
2 cloves roasted garlic
50 g Taleggio cheese
salt and pepper
1 dessertspoon olive oil

To roast the garlic, preheat the oven to 180°C. Break the cloves apart from the bulb – don't peel them – and place in a small ovenproof dish. Cover with oil and scatter over the herbs. Cover with foil and bake for 20 minutes. Cool and then peel the garlic. Strain over the oil (the oil is great in itself for garlic dressings) and set aside.

To prepare the steaks, preheat the oven to 180°C. Heat the oil in a frying pan. Season the steaks liberally with pepper and sprinkle with salt. When the pan is smoking, add the rib-eye steaks and seal on both sides for 1 minute each. Set aside to rest for 5 minutes.

Place 3 rashers of the pancetta on your board, slightly overlapping. Place a steak in the middle. Rub the thyme, rosemary and garlic onto the surface. Dot the Taleggio on top and roll the pancetta to envelop the steak.

Heat a frying pan until smoking hot and further seal the steaks on both sides until the pancetta is golden. Place on a roasting tray and bake for 10 minutes for medium rare, 15 for medium and 20–25 for well done. Rest for 2 minutes and serve.

roast baby beetroot

Serves 2

Beetroot baked in foil with onions, good red wine vinegar and thyme is a simple yet stunning prep-ahead vegetable.

8 baby beetroot, scrubbed
1 red onion
2 tablespoons red wine vinegar
2 tablespoons olive oil
1 teaspoon chopped fresh thyme
1 teaspoon caster sugar
1 teaspoon salt
freshly ground black pepper

Preheat the oven to 180°C. Take a sheet of foil and place the beetroot in the middle.

Peel the onion and cut into 8 wedges through the root. Scatter around the beetroot. Drizzle over the vinegar and oil. Scatter over the thyme, sugar and salt and season with five or six turns of black pepper. Gather up the foil to form a tight parcel and bake for 1 hour.

stuffed baby potatoes

Serves 2

I know life might be too short to stuff a baby potato, but there are only two of you, and what a wonderful way to say I love you!

8 medium-sized baby potatoes
2 chopped scallions
1 tablespoon chopped fresh chives
25 g sharp cheddar (or your favourite blue cheese)
2 tablespoons sour cream
salt and pepper to taste

Preheat the oven to 200°C.

Sprinkle the potatoes with salt and bake until soft, about 30 minutes. Cool slightly, then cut off the top third of the potato. Gently scoop out the potato from the centre with a teaspoon. Place the cooked potato into a bowl and add all the other ingredients. Mix well and season. Spoon this mixture back into the potatoes and top with the piece of potato sliced from the top. You can do this up to a day in advance. To reheat, bake in a 200°C preheated oven for 10 minutes.

red wine butter

Enough for 8 to 10 servings

It's awkward to make a small amount of this, so freeze what you don't need – it's great with barbecued steak, pork or oily fish.

2 shallots
2 cloves garlic
200 ml red wine
250 g butter at room temperature
handful of fresh chopped parsley

Chop the shallots and garlic finely and boil with the red wine until all but a tablespoon of liquid remains. Cool and blend with the butter until smooth. Fold in the parsley and then form into a sausage shape in cling film or greaseproof paper. Chill until solid and use as required.

scallion crêpes with five-spice duck

Serves 4

A crêpe lacks substance and so needs to be filled. This dish is an ideal way to celebrate Chinese New Year.

Crêpe batter:
125 g plain flour
3 finely chopped scallions
pinch salt
2 eggs
300 ml whole milk
25 g melted butter
oil or butter, for cooking

Five-spice blend
2 teaspoons fennel seeds
2 teaspoons Szechuan peppercorns
$\frac{1}{4}$ cinnamon stick
1 star anise
2 whole cloves

Duck breasts:
1 dessertspoon finely grated ginger
100 ml white wine or rice vinegar
1 tablespoon caster sugar
1 teaspoon salt
500 g duck breasts, fat scored
1 tablespoon vegetable oil
2 heads pak choy, leaves separated
1 tablespoon ginger, finely chopped
2 cloves crushed garlic
1 tablespoon sesame seeds
1 teaspoon sesame oil
1 bunch scallions
2 tablespoons hoisin sauce

To make the crêpes, sift the flour into a bowl and add the scallions and salt. Mix and then make a well in the centre. Add the eggs and milk and whisk together until smooth. Add the melted butter and set aside to rest.

Heat a frying pan or crêpe pan and when hot, lightly brush with oil or butter. Tilt the pan away from yourself and pour a ladle of the batter down the pan, swirling to cover the sides. Place directly on the heat and after 30 seconds, release from the sides with a palette knife. Flip over and cook for 30 seconds on the other side. Place on a piece of greaseproof paper and repeat, layering the crêpes between the paper to stop them sticking together.

To make the five-spice blend, blend all the ingredients together in a mortar and pestle or coffee grinder (just give this a good wash before grinding coffee in it) to a fine powder. Store in a plastic container or bag before use.

To prepare the duck breasts, boil the ginger, vinegar, sugar and salt for 20 seconds. Place the duck breast skin side down into the mixture and simmer for 2 minutes. Cool, then cover and refrigerate overnight. Remove from the vinegar and pat dry.

Sprinkle all over with a teaspoon of the five-spice blend and season with salt.

Place the duck, skin side down, in a dry, cold pan and cook slowly to render the fat, about 10 minutes on each side. Set aside to rest for 5 minutes, then shred finely.

Heat the vegetable oil in a wok and add the pak choy, ginger and garlic. Cook for 1 minute, then add the sesame seeds. When the seeds start to pop, add the sesame oil, scallions and hoisin sauce. Cook for 30 seconds and add to the shredded duck.

Place an equal amount of the duck mix in the middle of each pancake and fold over each corner to make a parcel. Serve straight away with extra hoisin for dipping.

triple gingerbread pancakes

Serves 4

That other February institution, Pancake Tuesday, is another great reason to celebrate. Let's face it, no matter how miserable you feel, flipping and dropping a pancake will always raise a smile. Serve these with maple syrup or the rum-soaked raisin and pear compote on p. 30 and the cinnamon mascarpone on p. 31.

3 eggs
200 ml buttermilk
1 tablespoon treacle
300 g plain flour
1 level teaspoon baking soda
1 teaspoon ground ginger
1 dessertspoon chopped preserved ginger
1 teaspoon chopped crystallised ginger
1 tablespoon caster sugar
zest of 1 lemon

Whisk the eggs, buttermilk and treacle together. Sift the flour and baking soda into a bowl with the three gingers, sugar and lemon zest. Make a well in the centre and add the buttermilk mixture and whisk to a smooth batter. Set aside for 20 minutes to rest.

Very lightly rub a griddle pan or frying pan with oil or butter and drop in tablespoons of the batter – keep them well apart, as they'll spread and rise. When bubbles appear on the surface, flip the pancakes over and cook for another minute on the other side. Cool on a wire rack or eat immediately with maple syrup or the rum-soaked raisin and pear compote on p. 30.

rum-soaked raisin and pear compote

Serves 8

I've always loved the combination of rum and raisins and this compote is perfect with the pancakes on p. 29. All it needs to make it a complete treat is a dollop of good-quality vanilla ice cream.

100 g raisins
100 ml golden rum or spiced rum, such as
  Morgan's Spiced Rum
4 ripe pears
25 g butter
1 teaspoon ground cinnamon
75 g light muscovado sugar

Soak the raisins in the rum overnight. Drain the raisins and set aside the rum. Peel the pears, quarter them, remove the core and then chop into 1 cm dice. Heat the butter in a pan over medium heat and add the pears and cinnamon. Cook for 5 minutes, then turn up the heat and add the rum and sugar. Simmer for 10 minutes, then add the raisins.

cinnamon mascarpone

Serves 8

Whipping sweet, creamy mascarpone cheese with spicy, warm cinnamon is a simple yet delicious topping for the pancakes on p. 29. It also goes well with the warm hazelnut cake and plums (p. 160) or Rachel's apple cider cake (p. 175).

2 teaspoons cinnamon
1 tablespoon maple syrup
250 g mascarpone cheese
200 ml double cream
1 tablespoon icing sugar

Heat the cinnamon and maple syrup together for 10 seconds. Allow to cool, then beat in the mascarpone. Fold in the cream and icing sugar.

This will keep in the fridge for up to 4 days.

poached rhubarb with lemongrass

Serves 2

For no other reason than rhubarb, I love February. Whoever the genius was who decided to plop a bucket on top of rhubarb shoots to fool them into growing quicker deserves to be sainted. Thin, beautifully pink, delicate stems of champagne or forced rhubarb elicit the most amorous reactions from even normally ice-cold rhubarb haters. They look and taste gorgeous. As rhubarb is Asian in origin, it does go beautifully with lemongrass.

Serve this with the cream cheese sorbet on p. 32 and the orange praline crumbs on p. 32.

100 g caster sugar
juice of 1 orange (retain the zest for the
   praline)
1 stalk lemongrass, finely chopped
50 ml water
4 stems of new season rhubarb

Boil the sugar, orange juice, lemongrass and water until the sugar dissolves. Cool in the pan and leave for at least 2 hours to diffuse.

Cut the rhubarb into 3 cm sticks and place in an ovenproof dish. Preheat the oven to 180°C.

Strain the sugar syrup over the rhubarb, place a sheet of greaseproof paper on top and cover tightly with tin foil. Bake for 30 minutes. Check the rhubarb is cooked by inserting a knife; it should be tender. Cool.

To serve, place some of the rhubarb at the bottom of a martini glass, top with a scoop of cream cheese sorbet (p. 32), top with more rhubarb and sprinkle with praline crumbs (p. 32).

cream cheese sorbet

Serves 6

Cream cheese frozen with a simple sugar syrup makes a great sorbet with a cheesecake feel.

200 ml water
200 g caster sugar
1 tablespoon glucose
juice and zest of 1 lemon
1 vanilla pod, split lengthwise and seeds
  scraped
250 g full-fat cream cheese (or 125 g cream
  cheese and 125 g mascarpone)

Boil the water, sugar, glucose, lemon zest and juice, vanilla pod and seeds until the sugar has dissolved. Cool and pass through a sieve. Wash and dry the vanilla pod in the oven and keep in a container of sugar – this will give you a jar of vanilla-infused sugar.

Blend the syrup and cream cheese in a liquidiser, then pour the mix into a shallow plastic tray. Freeze for 1 hour, then fluff with a fork. After 2 hours, blend the mix in a food processor and return to the tray. Freeze until solid. Remove from the freezer 10 minutes before serving.

orange praline crumbs

Serves 6

Caramelised almonds infused with orange and blitzed give a great texture and warmth to the poached rhubarb dish on p. 31. Leftover crumbs will keep in a sealed bag in a dry store for up to a month and are great served on ice cream or even your morning porridge.

200 g caster sugar
zest of 1 orange
50 g chopped almonds

In a heavy-based pan, heat the sugar over a high heat. Stir a little at the beginning, but when the sugar starts to break down don't touch it, as it will crystallise. When the sugar starts to colour, add the orange zest and cook until a rich amber colour. Add the nuts, then turn out onto a tray lined with non-stick parchment paper. Cool completely, then process to fine crumbs in a food processor, or place in a plastic bag and beat with a rolling pin.

a kitchen year

march

march

When I first started cooking professionally twenty years ago, Irish cuisine didn't really exist. Yes, we had stew, colcannon and champ, but nothing that would set the world on fire. Instead, chefs cooking in Ireland were like magpies, stealing from other country's repertoires. The first restaurant I worked in full time had a shipment delivered from Rungi's market in Paris every week. A polystyrene box would arrive full of quails, fresh herbs and exotic lettuces like oak leaf and radicchio.

I often think of that polystyrene box when I visit St George's market in Belfast, the Temple Bar Saturday market or the multitude of growers, cheese makers and artisan producers that I seek out throughout the year. A food revolution has swept through the island of Ireland. I think how exciting that box was to me then, a green-around-the-gills commis chef, and how it doesn't compare at all with the thrill I get at seeing what we're growing and producing now. Irish chefs who fled to find fantastic food elsewhere have returned home, realising the grass is most definitely not as green and lush on the other side – that's why we make the best cheese in the world!

That's why for March, to celebrate St Patrick, this chapter is dedicated to all things Irish – the cheese, spuds, vegetables, pork, bacon, apples and seafood. So raise a glass of the black stuff (or the golden) to the glorious present and the revolutionary future.

cashel Blue cheese soufflés with candied pecans and pears

Serves 4

Soufflés have all kinds of scary connotations, but twice baking them – once in a bain-marie and then again with a little cream and cheese – is an effective prepare-ahead, impressive dish. Candied pecans give an extra crunch, as do the pears, and both taste beautiful with the cheese. You can substitute any cheese for the Cashel Blue – I find this dish also works well with goat's cheese and Drumlin smoked cheese from Cavan.

Soufflés:
melted butter and breadcrumbs for lining the
  ramekins
1 tablespoon olive oil
1 small red onion, finely chopped
1 clove garlic, finely chopped
100 g butter
100 g plain flour
1 teaspoon finely chopped fresh rosemary
300 ml whole milk
200 g Cashel Blue cheese, grated
salt and pepper
2 large eggs, separated
50 ml double cream + 50 g extra Cashel Blue
  cheese

Candied pecans:
100 g sugar
1 tablespoon balsamic vinegar
100 g pecans

Pears:
1 tablespoon red wine vinegar
3 tablespoons olive oil
pinch caster sugar
pinch salt
3 turns fresh black pepper
1 tablespoon fresh chopped parsley leaves
2 ripe pears

mixed salad leaves, to serve

To make the soufflés, preheat the oven to 180°C. Brush 4 ramekins with melted butter, then scatter breadcrumbs in each to line. Tip out the excess breadcrumbs.

Heat the oil in a saucepan and add the onion and garlic. Cook until soft, then add the butter. When melted, beat in the flour and rosemary and then, on a low heat, add the milk a little at a time, beating as you go. When all the milk has been incorporated, cool slightly and then add the 200 g of Cashel cheese and season with salt and pepper.

Add the egg yolks to the cheese mixture and whisk the whites to stiff peaks. Gently fold the whites into the cheese mixture a tablespoon at a time. Pour the mixture into the ramekins and place in a roasting tin. Pour boiling water into the tray, halfway up the ramekins. Bake for 15 minutes. Cool and turn out onto a tray. You could make the soufflés to this stage 24 hours in advance.

When ready to serve, pour the cream and sprinkle the extra cheese over what was the bottom of the soufflé. Bake in an oven preheated to 200°C until golden and bubbling, about 10 minutes.

To make the candied pecans, heat the sugar and vinegar in a heavy-based saucepan, stirring only occasionally. When the sugar melts, cook on a high heat until it is runny and has caramelised. Add the nuts and pour onto a sheet of non-stick parchment paper to cool. When cold, break the nuts up with a strong knife and store in an airtight container until needed.

To make the pears, place the vinegar, oil, sugar, salt, pepper and parsley in a bowl and whisk together. Peel the pears, quarter and cut out the core. Slice each quarter into 3 slices and toss into the mixture.

To serve, place each soufflé into the middle of a bowl of mixed salad leaves. Arrange around the pears and scatter with the candied pecans. Drizzle with a little oil.

honey-cured pork loin with cider cream sauce

Serves 4

Curing meats in brine imparts them with a lovely juiciness when cooked. The more aromatics you add, the better, and honey and pork are a delicious combination. This cider sauce is a natural partner for pork, but is also good served with roast chicken.

Serve this with the baked stuffed onions with leeks and bacon on p. 40.

Honey-cured pork loin:
1 tablespoon crushed peppercorns
1 onion, roughly chopped
2 cloves garlic, chopped in their skins
500 ml water
4 tablespoons honey
100 g Demerara sugar
100 g sea salt
handful fresh rosemary, sage and thyme sprigs
1 kg piece pork loin, preferably organic

Cider cream sauce:
25 g butter
1 shallot, finely chopped
250 ml dry cider
250 ml chicken stock (see p. 11)
150 ml double cream
1 teaspoon fresh chopped thyme leaves
salt and pepper

Heat a dry saucepan and toast the peppercorns for 30 seconds. Add all the other ingredients except the pork and simmer until the sugar has dissolved. Cool completely. Score the fat on the pork and pour the brine over the top, ensuring the joint is completely submerged. Chill for at least 24 hours and up to 48 hours.

Preheat the oven to 200°C. Remove the pork from the brine and pat dry. Heat a frying pan and when hot add the pork, fat side down. Cook until golden, about 2 minutes, then flip over and seal on all sides. Place in a roasting tin and cover with foil or in a casserole with a lid and cook for 1 hour, or until an inserted skewer comes out hot and the internal temperature reads at least 70°C. Rest for 10 minutes and slice.

To make the cider cream sauce, heat the butter in a saucepan over a medium heat and add the shallot. Cook until soft and add the cider. Crank up the heat to full and boil to reduce the liquid by half. Add the stock and boil this to reduce by half again. Add the cream and boil and reduce until the liquid has the consistency of single cream. Strain through a sieve and add the thyme leaves. Check for seasoning.

baked stuffed onions with leeks and bacon

Serves 4

4 medium onions
2 rashers dry-cured streaky bacon, cut into 1
  cm pieces
25 g butter
100 g finely chopped leeks
salt and pepper
100 ml double cream
50 g grated local cheddar

Preheat the oven to 200°C.

Peel the onions, leaving the root intact. Place in a saucepan, cover with water, season with salt and simmer gently until soft, or until an inserted knife comes out easily. Drain and cool.

Place the onions root side down on a surface and carefully hollow out each onion with a sharp knife. Chop the inside of the onion. Heat a pan until hot and add the bacon, cooking until crisp. Remove the bacon from the pan, lower the heat and add the butter. Add the chopped onion and leeks, season with a little salt and pepper, and cook until soft. Add the cream and reduce by half. Add the cooked bacon and spoon into the hollowed-out onions. Sprinkle with cheese and bake for 15 minutes.

colcannon

Serves 4

Everybody has their own personal favourite way of cooking this dish. I like to fry thinly shredded savoy cabbage in butter and then fold that into fluffy mashed potatoes with a cream and milk mixture that's been infused with chopped scallions. Whatever way you serve it, I think it's imperative that you form it into a big mound and make a well in the centre for a golden pool of melted butter.

1 kg floury potatoes
½ savoy cabbage
50 g butter
salt and pepper
100 ml double cream
4 scallions, chopped
50 g butter, to serve

Boil the potatoes in their jackets until they're soft.

Quarter and remove the core from the cabbage, then shred as thinly as possible. Heat the butter in a large saucepan and add the cabbage, ½ teaspoon of salt and a few grinds of black pepper. Cook until the cabbage is soft, about 5 minutes.

Drain the potatoes and peel them while hot, then press through a potato ricer. Place the cream and scallions in a large saucepan and bring to the boil. Add the riced potatoes and cooked cabbage and stir until hot.

To serve, mound the potato mixture into a bowl, make a well in the centre and add the final 50 g of butter.

seafood and bacon hotpot

Serves 4

I have fond memories of the many Lancashire hotpots I had when living in the north of England. I love the combination of warm stew topped with crisp, cooked potatoes. Using fish instead of lamb makes for a lighter version. Bacon and seafood are a natural combination anyway and the golden potato crust tops the whole thing off.

1 kg mixed scrubbed cockles and mussels
100 ml dry cider
150 g dry-cured streaky bacon, cut into 1 cm
  strips
25 g butter
1 onion, finely chopped
100 g celery, finely chopped
2 cloves garlic, finely chopped
200 ml double cream
750 g firm fish fillets, cut into 3 cm chunks
  (monkfish, cod, gurnard, haddock, smoked
  cod or smoked haddock are all good)
500 g peeled potatoes, sliced ½ cm thick,
  boiled in salted water until cooked and
  drained
50 g grated smoked Gubbeen cheese
salt and pepper

Ensure the shells of the cockles and mussels are tightly shut, otherwise throw them out.

Heat a large saucepan until hot and add the cider. Add the cockles and mussels, cover with a lid and cook for 2 to 3 minutes, or until the shells start to open. Strain over a bowl to catch the cooking liquid. Remove the meat from the shells and set aside.

Heat an ovenproof casserole dish over high heat and add the bacon. Cook until golden. Add the butter, onion, celery and garlic to the pan and cook on a low heat for 10 minutes, stirring occasionally. Add the reserved cooking liquid from the shellfish and simmer for 5 minutes. Add the cream and simmer for 5 minutes. Check for seasoning. Add the chunks of fish fillets and cook for 3 minutes on a gentle simmer. Check that the fish is firm to the touch, with a little give. Add the cooked cockles and mussels.

Remove from the heat and arrange the hot, sliced potatoes on top. Top with the grated Gubbeen and grill until golden and bubbling. Serve immediately with bread. (The wheaten farls on p. 42 would be ideal.)

wheaten farls

Serves 4

This recipe is from my friend Jane McAuley, a terrific natural baker who never weighs anything. If you're like me, I suggest you actually weigh the ingredients! Farls are a quick, simple peasant bread cooked in a griddle pan. There's no proving required and they are fantastic split open straight off the griddle and dripping with butter.

200 g wheaten flour
100 g plain flour
1 level teaspoon baking soda
½ teaspoon salt
250 ml buttermilk

Mix the flours, baking soda and salt in a bowl and make a well in the centre. Add the buttermilk and mix to a sticky dough. Turn onto a floured surface and knead for 30 seconds. Roll into a big ball and then roll out to a 10 cm round. Divide into quarters.

Lightly dust a frying pan or griddle pan with flour and add the farls. Cook for 8 minutes on each side.

steamed apple and whiskey puddings with honeycomb cream

Serves 4

Steamed puddings are a true joy. Eat this pudding and the world will seem a better, simpler place.

Honeycomb cream:
200 ml double cream
4 tablespoons store-bought honeycomb

Puddings:
25 g raisins
good glug whiskey
1 tablespoon honey
100 g butter, softened to room temperature
100 g light muscovado sugar
2 small eggs
100 g self-raising flour
¼ teaspoon baking powder
½ teaspoon mixed spice
50 g cooking apple, peeled and core removed
15 g caster sugar

To make the honeycomb cream, lightly whip the cream to soft peaks and fold in the honeycomb. Set aside.

To make the puddings, butter 4 individual pudding moulds or ramekins. Soak the raisins in the whiskey for 2 hours, then boil with the honey until the liquid has evaporated. Set aside.

Beat the butter and sugar until light and fluffy, then add the eggs a little at a time. Sift in the flour, baking powder and spice and mix well.

Chop the apple into 1 cm dice and toss in the caster sugar. Fold into the batter with the raisins. Pour into the moulds, cover loosely with tin foil and place in a steamer for 30 minutes. Turn out and serve as soon as possible with the honeycomb cream.

savoury biscuits to go with cheese

Makes 20 biscuits

These biscuits are a good way of using up cheese leftover from a dinner party cheeseboard. They're best made with a hard cheese – these days, there are so many good artisan cheeses in Ireland, you'll be spoiled for choice. They'll keep in an airtight tin for up to a week – that is, if you ever get as far as cooling them! Serve these with cheese and the sweet sour grapes on p. 46.

100 g softened butter
100 g plain flour
65 g finely grated hard cheese
1 egg yolk

Mix all the ingredients in a food processor to a smooth dough. Wrap in cling film and chill for 10 minutes. Line baking trays with non-stick parchment paper and preheat the oven to 180°C.

Roll the dough out to ¼ cm thick and cut into desired shapes. Place on baking trays and cook until golden, about 12 minutes. Cool on wire racks and serve with your favourite cheeses.

sweet sour grapes

Serves 4

A change from the usual chutney to go with cheese. Serve these alongside the savoury biscuits on p. 45.

250 g red seedless grapes
100 ml port
50 g caster sugar
1 tablespoon white balsamic vinegar

Heat a large saucepan or frying pan until smoking hot and add the grapes. Cook for 1 minute, then add the port, sugar and vinegar. Boil for 20 minutes, or until the liquid is thick and syrupy. Cool and place in a container. This will keep in the fridge for up to a month.

a kitchen year

april

april

Even if it's chucking it down in sub-zero temperatures, at its heart there is that feeling of freshness and new life around April. I'm no gardener, but I always get a warm glow when I notice the first mint sprigs appearing in the pot at the back door.

New season cheeses that are appearing around this time have a tongue-tingling zing that says spring like nothing else. Except, that is, for the tender, sweet lamb that is so succulent right now. Nothing says winter's over like the combination of these two things.

Although we're getting into summer mode this month, I think it's still appropriate to spice things up. Oily mackerel is superb at the moment and should be enjoyed as spankingly fresh as possible. Giving it a taste and flavour injection of Moroccan spices will pep you up no end and get those creaky winter joints jolted back into action.

In this chapter, there's an Easter lunch menu that combines lamb with mint, lemon and almonds, enveloped in buttery, freshly baked brioche dough. And what better way to finish than with a glowing lemon cake, made even mellower with the addition of some polenta and topped with an orange frosting.

moroccan-spiced mackerel

Serves 4

My favourite way of eating mackerel is straight off the boat (preferably caught myself) and simply grilled on a barbecue with a squeeze of lemon. Doing this on a cold, Irish April day isn't really feasible, but pairing mackerel with sunny Moroccan flavours is. Throw in a spicy, sweet carrot salad with creamy chickpeas (p. 53) and crisp flatbread (p. 52) and who needs summer?

8 mackerel fillets, pin boned

Spice blend:
10 cardamom pods
2 teaspoons coriander seeds
2 teaspoons fennel seeds
2 teaspoons cumin seeds
zest of 1 orange
1 teaspoon smoked paprika
4 tablespoons olive oil

Crack the cardamoms to release the seeds. Place the cardamom seeds with the other seeds in a mortar and pestle or coffee grinder and process to a fine powder. Set aside half this mixture for the carrot salad on p. 53, if making. Combine the remaining spices with the orange zest, smoked paprika and olive oil. Rub all over the mackerel and set aside for 1 hour.

To cook the mackerel, heat a griddle pan or frying pan until smoking hot. (Alternatively, weather permitting, light the barbecue.) Season the mackerel with salt on both sides and place, skin side down, on the pan. Cook for 2 minutes, or until you can actually see the mackerel cooking up the sides. Flip over and cook for 2 minutes on the other side. Serve immediately.

flatbread

Serves 8

These crispy flatbreads are the perfect contrast to the soft mackerel on p. 50 and creamy chickpeas on p. 53. They would also go well with the tandoori chicken on p. 135 or the butternut squash fritters on p. 132.

150 g plain flour
125 g wholemeal flour
1 teaspoon salt
1 tablespoon natural yoghurt
1 tablespoon olive oil
100 ml water

Place the flours and salt in a bowl. In a separate bowl, whisk the yoghurt, oil and water together and mix to a dough with the flour mix. Wrap in cling film and chill for 20 minutes.

Divide the dough into 8 pieces. Roll each piece in a ball and roll on a lightly floured surface into a 2-mm thick round (don't worry about perfect circles, this is a rustic bread). Heat a griddle or frying pan over a medium-high heat and add a prepared flatbread. When the surface starts to bubble, turn over and cook for 30 seconds on the other side. Repeat with the other breads and stack them as you go.

spiced carrot and chickpea salad

This salad is ideal with the Moroccan-spiced mackerel on p. 50, but also works well with salmon and grilled chicken.

If you're making this to serve with the Moroccan-spiced mackerel on p. 50, you can use half of the mixture of cardamom, coriander seeds, fennel seeds and cumin seeds from that recipe for this one. Otherwise, if you're making this salad on its own, use the amounts listed here.

4 tablespoons olive oil
2 large carrots, peeled and grated
5 cardamom pods
1 teaspoons coriander seeds
2 teaspoons fennel seeds
1 teaspoons cumin seeds
2 cloves garlic, crushed
1 tablespoon finely grated ginger
1 tablespoon sesame seeds
2 lemons
100 ml mayonnaise
100 ml natural yoghurt
1 x 400 g tin chickpeas, drained
1 red onion, peeled and finely sliced
handful fresh coriander, chopped roughly

Heat the oil in a large frying pan over a high heat. When hot, add the carrots and cook until golden.

Crack the cardamoms to release the seeds. Place the cardamom seeds with the other seeds in a mortar and pestle or coffee grinder and process to a fine powder. Add the ground spices, garlic and ginger to the carrots and cook for 1 minute. Set aside in a bowl.

Clean out the pan, heat until smoking and dry toast the sesame seeds in the pan until they start to pop. Set aside.

Cut the lemons in half and brush with oil on the cut side. Heat the pan until smoking hot and cook the lemons, flesh side down, until golden, about 1 minute. Squeeze the juice into a bowl and whisk in the mayonnaise and yoghurt. Toss this dressing into the carrot mixture and add the sesame seeds, chickpeas, red onion and coriander.

tostadas with goat's cheese-stuffed piquillos and roasted almond and parsley dressing

Serves 4

Making soft flour tortillas might seem like a lot of bother for little reward, but trust me, the effort is well worth it. Whenever I make these tortillas, everyone who eats them agrees that they're a thousand miles away from their pre-made, pre-packed namesakes. To make them into tostadas, simply press into a cake tin or metal frying pan and bake in an oven at 200°C for 5 minutes, or until they're crisp.

Piquillo peppers are delicious, chestnut wood-roasted baby peppers that have a slight kick when you eat them. Their natural smoky spiciness cuts through soft goat's cheese. Toasted almonds give the whole dish a crunch in this rustic dressing. April is an ideal month for sampling fresh goat's cheese – there are many gorgeous varieties scattered around Ireland.

The roasted almond and parsley dressing is a rustic dressing – the nuts provide a great texture balance with the smooth goat's cheese. A drop of honey in the dressing will cut through the natural 'sting' of the goat's cheese.

Goat's cheese-stuffed piquillos:
1 tablespoon olive oil
2 shallots, peeled and finely chopped
2 cloves garlic, crushed
6 sunblush tomatoes
200 g goat's cheese
100 ml double cream
handful of finely chopped flat leaf parsley
salt and pepper
8 piquillo peppers, whole

Roasted almond dressing:
100 g flaked almonds
handful of fresh chopped flat leaf parsley
2 cloves roasted garlic (see p. 8)
1 tablespoon honey
juice of 1 lemon
100 ml extra virgin olive oil
2 finely chopped piquillo peppers
salt and pepper

Tostadas:
4 soft flour tortillas (make up half the amount of dough on p. 9 and use the same method)
assorted salad leaves, such as mizuna and rocket

To make the goat's cheese mousse, heat the oil in a pan and cook the shallots and garlic until golden brown. Cool, then process with the sunblush tomatoes and goat's cheese to a smooth paste. Fold in the cream and parsley and season with salt and pepper. Spoon the mousse into the whole piquillos and chill on a tray for 1 hour.

To make the dressing, toast the almonds on a tray in the oven until golden brown. Cool slightly and chop on a board with the parsley. Place the garlic in a bowl and smash with a fork. Whisk in the almond mixture, honey and lemon juice. Add the oil and peppers and season well.

To assemble the tostadas, scatter the leaves over each tortilla and place 2 stuffed peppers in the middle. Drizzle over the dressing.

stuffed loin of lamb baked in brioche, with red wine gravy

Serves 4

Serve this with the creamed flageolet beans on p. 58.

Loin of lamb:
1 tablespoon olive oil
250 g fresh spinach
salt and pepper
25 g butter
1 onion, finely chopped
4 cloves garlic, finely chopped
2 tablespoons double cream
25 g pine nuts
25 g breadcrumbs
zest of 1 lemon
handful of fresh chopped mint leaves
2 deboned racks of lamb (your butcher will do this for you) – keep the bones for stock for the gravy
oil, for cooking

Brioche:
250 g strong bread flour
1 x 7 g sachet yeast
½ teaspoon salt
1 dessertspoon caster sugar
3 large eggs, lightly beaten
125 g softened butter
1 egg yolk, beaten

Red wine gravy:
bones from the deboned rack of lamb
1 carrot, roughly chopped
1 onion, roughly chopped
1 stick celery, roughly chopped
1 tablespoon tomato purée
sprigs of fresh rosemary and thyme
6 crushed peppercorns
25 g butter
½ carrot, chopped into small dice
1 stick celery, chopped into small dice
1 onion, finely chopped
350 ml rich red wine, such as a Shiraz
salt and pepper

To prepare the loin of lamb, preheat the oven to 180°C. Heat the oil in a large pan and add the spinach. Season well and turn around in the pan so it wilts. When cooked down, squeeze in a sieve to remove all the moisture and chop roughly.

Heat the butter in a pan and sweat off the onion and garlic. Add the cream and remove from the heat.

Toast the pine nuts in a dry frying pan until golden brown. Chop finely and mix in with the spinach mixture. Add the breadcrumbs, lemon zest and mint. Mix and check the seasoning.

Season the lamb with salt and pepper. Heat a pan until smoking. Lightly oil the lamb and add to the pan. Cook for 2 minutes on each side. Remove from the pan and leave to rest. Pat dry with kitchen paper, then top each piece of lamb with the stuffing.

To make the brioche, place the flour, yeast, salt and sugar in the bowl of a food mixer with the dough hook attached. Process on a low speed and slowly add the eggs in a steady stream. When smooth, beat in the butter a tablespoon at a time. When incorporated fully, mix for a further 5 minutes. Cover with cling film and leave for 1 hour. After an hour, knock back the dough and place in the fridge, still covered, for 1 hour – this will make it easier to roll.

Divide the dough in half and roll each piece into a sausage shape on a floured surface. Roll the sausage into a rectangle. Place the lamb in the middle and brush round the edges with the beaten egg yolk. Fold into a parcel. Brush all over with more egg yolk. Repeat with the other loin. Bake the lamb for 30 minutes and allow to rest.

To make the red wine gravy, first make the lamb stock. Roast the bones in a 200°C oven until dark but not burned. Pour off the oil from the roasting tray into a large saucepan. Heat the oil and cook off the vegetables until golden. Add the tomato purée and cook for 2 minutes. Add the roasted bones, herbs and peppercorns and cover with cold water. Bring to the boil and simmer for 4 hours. You may need to add more water to the stock. Strain the liquid, place the lamb stock in a saucepan and boil until reduced by half, about 1 litre (if there's any left, freeze it in bags).

Heat the butter in a saucepan over a medium heat and add the carrots, celery and onion. Cook until golden and soft. Crank up the heat and add the red wine and boil until it is reduced by half. Add the reduced stock and boil until reduced to a syrupy gravy. Strain and check the seasoning.

After the lamb has rested, slice each parcel into 4 pieces. Serve on a platter with a jug of the red wine gravy on the side.

creamed flageolet beans

Serves 4

Flageolet beans are a much underused pulse. They have a fresh pea-like quality when cooked. Add rosemary to the mix and you have a perfect accompaniment to lamb.

250 g dried flageolet beans
1 litre chicken stock (see p. 11)
sprigs of fresh rosemary and thyme
2 whole garlic cloves
25 g butter
1 tablespoon olive oil
1 onion, chopped finely
100 g chopped leeks
100 ml double cream
1 tablespoon fresh chopped rosemary
salt and pepper
fresh chopped flat leaf parsley

Soak the beans in cold water overnight. Drain the beans and wash under cold water. Place in a saucepan with the chicken stock, herb sprigs and garlic. Bring to the boil and simmer until soft – this will vary, but will take at least 30 minutes. When done, drain the beans but keep the cooking liquid.

Heat the butter and oil together in a saucepan over a medium heat and add the onion and leeks. Cook until golden and add 500 ml of the bean cooking liquid. Boil to reduce by half and then add the cream and rosemary. Boil to reduce the liquid to a consistency of single cream. Fold in the cooked beans and check seasoning. Add the parsley and serve.

focaccia with oregano,
feta and olives

Serves 4

Freshly baked focaccia bread, springy from the olive oil in the dough, is the perfect vehicle for feta cheese, herbs and olives. Buy the best olives you can (you'd be better off using fewer olives than cheaper varieties). This bread is nearly a meal in itself but would be great with the tostadas on p. 55 as a light supper.

1 kg strong bread flour
1 teaspoon salt
2 x 7 g sachets yeast
2 cloves roasted garlic (see p. 8)
100 ml olive oil
150 ml white wine
500 ml lukewarm water
handful of fresh chopped oregano (use basil if
   you can't get fresh oregano)
1 punnet cherry tomatoes, halved
100 g feta cheese
100 g mixed black and green olives
sea salt and good olive oil, for garnish

Place the flour, salt and yeast in a bowl. Crush the roasted garlic and mix with the olive oil, wine and water and half the chopped oregano. Add to the flour mixture. Mix to a sticky dough, then turn onto a floured surface and knead for 10 minutes. Place in a lightly oiled bowl, cover with a damp tea towel and leave for 1 hour.

Preheat the oven to 190°C. Press the dough into a floured baking tray. Press all over the surface with your fingertips to make indents. Place the cherry tomatoes, flesh side up, all over the dough. Season the top of the tomatoes with some sea salt. Crumble the feta over the top and scatter over the olives. Leave for 10 minutes. Bake for 20 minutes, or until golden and firm. Remove from the oven and mix the remaining oregano with 4 tablespoons of olive oil and drizzle over the top. Slice into wedges and serve.

sticky lemon polenta cake with orange frosting

Serves 4

Polenta cake:

150 g butter at room temperature

200 g caster sugar + 75 g caster sugar (for
   lemon syrup)

4 eggs

150 g plain flour

1 teaspoon baking powder

100 g ground almonds

100 g polenta

2 tablespoons sour cream

zest of 2 lemons (retain the juice)

Orange frosting:

1 vanilla pod, split

zest and juice of 2 oranges

100 g caster sugar

50 g chopped white chocolate

200 g mascarpone cheese

200 ml double cream

To make the cake, preheat the oven to 180°C.
Beat the butter and 200 g of caster sugar until
pale and fluffy. Add the eggs, one at a time. Sift
the flour and baking powder together and mix
with the ground almonds and polenta. Fold into
the egg mixture. Add the sour cream and lemon
zest. Pour into a greased 10-inch cake tin, the
bottom lined with non-stick parchment paper.
Bake for 30 to 40 minutes, or until an inserted
skewer comes out clean.

Remove the cake from the oven. Pierce the cake all
over with a skewer while still in the tin. Boil the
retained lemon juice and 75 g of sugar together
until they form a syrup with a pouring consistency.
Pour this syrup all over the cake. Remove the cake
from the tin and allow to cool.

To make the frosting, split the vanilla pod, scrape
the seeds into a saucepan and add the pod. Add
the zest and juice of the oranges and the sugar.
Simmer until the sugar dissolves. Remove from the
heat and strain into a bowl.

While still hot, stir in the chocolate. Cool slightly,
then whisk the orange mixture with the
mascarpone. Fold in the cream. Spread over the
lemon cake and serve immediately.

a kitchen year

may

may

One of the best things about living in Ireland is the clearly defined seasons. Friends who've moved to America or Australasia moan about missing two things – city breaks in Europe and changes in the weather!

May can have every season crammed into one day – I've known snow in May and scorching heat as well. For this reason, the recipes in this chapter lean towards what's best about Italian cuisine – some salad, pizza and pasta, but also comfort food in the form of a creamy corn soup, risotto and rice pudding.

I love the style of Mediterranean food, but I'm more passionate about local produce and I think this chapter makes the most of both. We might not have the olive oil, but our meat, fish and dairy produce are the best in the world.

As is our beer – I used to make beer bread rolls so often that I sickened myself and then stopped making them completely! But, as with so many other things, absence makes the heart grow fonder and my friends eventually persuaded me to reinstate them to their former glory. They're rich, spongy rolls – the combination of beer and eggs achieves this – and I'll be eternally grateful to their persistent champions for rekindling my love for them. They are a fantastic bread to mop up all the sumptuous sauces in this chapter.

rotolo filled with spinach, roasted red peppers and oregano

Serves 4

Making your own pasta may seem tedious, but it truly is very satisfying and well worth the effort. Alternatively, you can find fresh pasta sheets in most supermarkets and delis.

Rotolo literally means 'rolled'. Poached lasagne sheets are spread with filling and rolled up like a Swiss roll. These are either pan fried or baked with cheese. Either way, they make a refreshing change to mundane, clichéd pasta dishes.

Serve with mixed salad leaves and the smoked tomato salsa on p. 71.

Fresh pasta dough:
200 g '00' pasta flour
½ teaspoon salt
5 large egg yolks
1 dessertspoon olive oil

Filling:
2 red peppers
olive oil
10 g butter
200 g spinach
200 g ricotta cheese
2 red onions, finely sliced
2 cloves garlic, finely chopped
1 tablespoon chopped fresh oregano
25 g grated Parmesan
1 egg yolk
salt and pepper

mixed salad leaves, to serve

To make the pasta, sift the flour and salt into a bowl or food processor. Mix in the egg yolks and oil and enough water to make a stiff but not dry dough. Wrap in cling film and chill for 20 minutes.

Roll the dough into a sausage and set your pasta roller to its widest setting. Roll the sausage into a rectangle thin enough to fit into the setting. Roll through the pasta roller twice. Turn the setting down to the next thickest setting and repeat the rolling. Do this until you've reached the next to last setting, then cut into 4 equal sheets.

Poach in simmering salted water for 2 minutes. Drain, cool under cold water and pat dry with kitchen towels.

To make the filling, preheat the oven to 200°C. Brush the red peppers with oil and season with salt. Roast in the oven until scorched, about 30 minutes. Place in a plastic bag and leave for 5 minutes, then peel and deseed the peppers.

Heat the butter in a large saucepan and add the spinach. Season and cook until wilted. Squeeze the spinach in a sieve until all the liquid is removed. Chop and place in a bowl and mix in the ricotta.

Heat 1 tablespoon of oil in a frying pan and add the onions and garlic. Cook over a medium heat until soft and golden. Allow to cool slightly and add to the spinach mixture. Chop the peppers and add to the mix, along with the oregano and Parmesan cheese. Check the seasoning.

Take a lasagne sheet and lay it flat on a sheet of cling film. Brush the top edge of the lasagne sheet (about 1 cm from the edge) with egg yolk, then spread a quarter of the spinach mixture over the rest of the lasagne. Take the end closest to you and roll up towards the egg yolk end, keeping the cling film around the roll of pasta. Repeat with the other sheets and chill for 1 hour.

Remove the cling film and slice each roll into 5 cylinders. Either heat 2 tablespoons of oil in a frying pan and cook the rotolo until golden brown all over, or place in an oiled baking dish, sprinkle with fresh grated Parmesan and bake in a 200°C oven for 10 minutes.

Serve with salad leaves and the smoked tomato salsa on p. 71.

smoked tomato salsa

Makes 250 g

There's something about sweet, juicy cherry tomatoes that makes them ideal for smoking. The balance of flavours is lovely – smoky and sweet with a dash of sourness from the vinegar and fresh and vibrant with the basil. This salsa would also work well with grilled meats, chicken, oily fish or grilled goat's cheese.

250 g cherry tomatoes
½ teaspoon caster sugar
salt and pepper
1 tablespoon olive oil
2 shallots, peeled and finely chopped
1 clove garlic, crushed
1 tablespoon red wine vinegar
handful fresh chopped basil
3 tablespoons extra virgin olive oil
salt and pepper

Preheat the oven to 200°C.

Line a roasting tin with tin foil. Scatter some wood chips in the tin and place a cooling rack on top. Cut the tomatoes in half and place on the rack. Sprinkle over the sugar and season with salt and pepper. Cover tightly with foil and place the tray on a cooker ring on full heat (turn the extractor on) or do on a barbecue outside. Cook for 2 minutes. Cool and remove the foil, then place the tomatoes on a lightly oiled tray and bake for 10 minutes.

Heat the olive oil in a saucepan and cook the shallots and garlic on a low heat until soft. Add the vinegar and cooked smoked tomatoes until they are heated through. Remove from the heat and add the basil and extra virgin oil. Season with salt and pepper.

luxurious macaroni and cheese

Serves 4

Nothing says comfort food like mac and cheese. I loved this dish as a child – the smell of melted cheese alone is sublime – but this is a grown-up version. The béchamel is replaced with a creamy mascarpone sauce and smoked pancetta and sweet Borettane onions add an adult feel.

225 g penne or orzo pasta
1 teaspoon salt
1 tablespoon olive oil
6 rashers of smoked pancetta or good-quality smoked streaky bacon, chopped into 1 cm cubes
25 g butter
1 medium onion, thinly sliced
2 cloves garlic, chopped finely
100 ml dry white wine
100 g Borettane onions, chopped
1 tablespoon fresh chopped rosemary
salt and pepper
350 ml double cream
75 g fresh spinach, washed
75 g grated Parmesan cheese
100 g mascarpone cheese
100 g Fontina cheese

Preheat the oven to 200°C.

Bring a large pot of water to a rolling boil and add the pasta and 1 teaspoon of salt. Cook for 5 minutes, then drain and toss in the oil.

Heat a large frying pan until hot and add the pancetta or bacon. Cook until golden, then remove from the pan and set aside. Pour off any fat from the pan and add the butter. Turn the heat down to medium hot and add the onion and garlic. Cook until golden and add the wine, Borettane onions and rosemary. Simmer for 5 minutes and season well with salt and pepper. Add the cream and simmer until the mixture has the consistency of single cream. Add the spinach and stir until it has wilted. Add the cooked pancetta, cooked pasta, Parmesan and mascarpone cheese. Check the seasoning and remove from the heat.

Place the mixture in an ovenproof dish and grate over the Fontina cheese (use Taleggio or a sharp cheddar if you can't get Fontina) and bake for 20 minutes.

pizza bianco with smoked beef, red wine shallots and Gorgonzola

Serves 4

Pizza bianco is literally 'white pizza' – it has a white sauce rather than the traditional red. If smoking the beef is too time consuming, then substitute Parma ham or grilled beef – the effect is equally stunning. This pizza dough is the result of a lot of experimentation over the years. For perfect results, type '00' flour is the best (available in good delis and supermarkets). Add a tablespoon of honey to the dough for a lovely, golden crust.

Oak chips can be bought in hardware/DIY shops or in the barbecue section of supermarkets.

Pizza dough:
350 g '00' flour
1 teaspoon salt
1 x 7 g sachet dried yeast
300 ml lukewarm water
1 tablespoon honey
1 tablespoon olive oil

Smoked sirloin of beef:
200 g oak chips soaked in cold water
250 g sirloin of beef
salt and pepper
1 tablespoon olive oil

Red wine shallots:
1 tablespoon olive oil
4 shallots, peeled and finely sliced
100 ml red wine
1 tablespoon red wine vinegar
1 tablespoon caster sugar
1 teaspoon fresh chopped thyme
salt and pepper

White sauce (also known as Alfredo sauce):
125 ml double cream
1 clove garlic, crushed
30 g fresh grated Parmesan

100g Gorgonzola, crumbled
rocket leaves, to serve

To make the dough, mix the flour, salt and yeast in a bowl and make a well in the centre. Add the water, honey and olive oil and mix to a loose dough. Turn onto a floured board and knead for 5 to 10 minutes, or until the dough starts to feel elastic when pulled apart. Place in a lightly oiled bowl covered with a damp tea towel and leave for 1 hour.

Meanwhile, to make the beef, drain the oak chips well. Line a roasting tin with tin foil and sprinkle the soaked chips over the bottom. Place a wire rack on top. Season the sirloin well and place on the rack. Cover tightly with foil. Place directly on top of a cooker ring and cook on full heat for 2 minutes. Cool and remove the foil. Heat a pan until smoking hot and add the oil. Pat the sirloin dry and seal on both sides for 2 minutes. Cool and slice thinly.

To make the red wine shallots, heat the oil in a saucepan over a medium heat and add the shallots. Cook for 10 minutes, then add the remaining ingredients. Simmer until all the liquid has disappeared, about 10 minutes. Check the seasoning.

To make the white sauce, boil the cream and garlic together for 1 minute. Remove from the heat and stir in the Parmesan.

To assemble, preheat the oven to 210°C and place a baking sheet in the oven.

Meanwhile, turn the dough onto a surface and knock out the air with your fist. Roll the dough as thinly as you can, ensuring it will fit the baking sheet. Take the hot tray from the oven and sprinkle it lightly with flour or polenta. Place the dough on top and spread the sauce all over, leaving a 1 cm margin at the edges. Top with the beef, scatter over the onions and dot with 100 g crumbled Gorgonzola. Bake for 10 minutes, or until the crust is golden and the cheese is bubbling.

Serve the pizza on a plate with a little lightly dressed rocket scattered over the top.

plum tomatoes filled with tomato and lovage risotto

Serves 4

Stuffed plum tomatoes might have a bit of a Seventies vibe, but filling tangy ripe tomatoes with creamy risotto is a timeless classic. Lovage is a medieval herb that has a flavour and aroma like intense celery. It gives the tomatoes and rice a really savoury feel.

Risotto takes a bit of time to prepare, though slowly adding the stock to the rice and stirring as you go is well worth the effort. You could make the tomatoes up in advance and store in the fridge.

6 large plum tomatoes

Cooking liquid for risotto:
flesh from tomatoes above
200 ml dry white wine
500 ml water
stalks from the handful of lovage below
1 onion, finely chopped
2 cloves garlic, sliced
1 teaspoon salt

Tomato and lovage risotto:
1 tablespoon olive oil
1 shallot, peeled and finely chopped
1 clove garlic, finely chopped
100 g arborio or carnaroli rice
splash of white wine or Noilly Prat vermouth
400 ml cooking liquid (above)
handful of chopped lovage leaves
20 g butter
50 g grated Parmesan
salt and pepper

To prepare the tomatoes, cut the bottoms off them, being careful not to cut into the flesh. Cut the top off each tomato and scoop the flesh from the inside. Reserve the flesh for the cooking liquid for the risotto.

To make the cooking liquid, place everything in a saucepan, bring to the boil and simmer for 20 minutes. Leave to infuse.

To make the risotto, heat the oil in a saucepan and add the shallot and garlic. Cook on a low heat until soft, about 5 minutes. Add the rice and cook until it becomes translucent, about 2 minutes. Add the wine or vermouth and stir until it disappears. Add a ladle full of cooking liquid and cook, stirring constantly, until the liquid has evaporated. Repeat this until the risotto has absorbed the liquid and has a little bite when tasted. Add the lovage, butter and Parmesan and remove from the heat. Spoon the risotto into the tomato shells in a lightly oiled ovenproof baking dish.

To finish, preheat the oven to 200°C. Drizzle the tomatoes with a little oil and season with salt and pepper and bake for 10 minutes.

lemon and white chocolate rice pudding with peach, limoncello and honey compote

Serves 4

Rice pudding evokes fantastic memories of childhood, but this is a mature, decadent version that makes me glad I'm older. The recipe makes six individual puddings, so if there are four of you, you can fight over the last two!

Candied lemon and white chocolate rice pudding:
100 g short-grain pudding rice (arborio rice also works well)
50 g caster sugar + 100 g caster sugar for candied layer
250 ml whole milk
250 ml double cream
15 g butter
50 g chopped good-quality white chocolate
zest of 1 lemon (save the juice for the compote)
2 large eggs, separated
butter, for greasing

Peach, limoncello and honey compote:
4 ripe peaches
2 tablespoons honey
50 g caster sugar
2 tablespoons water
1 vanilla pod
juice of the lemon from above
50 ml limoncello

To make the puddings, preheat the oven to 180°C. Lightly butter 6 ramekins and sprinkle with a little sugar and swirl round to coat the inside.

Wash the rice and place in a saucepan with the 50 g of caster sugar, milk, cream and butter. Bring to the boil, cover and simmer gently for 20 minutes – the rice should have soaked up all the liquid and be soft. Remove from the heat, fold in the white chocolate and lemon zest and allow to cool.

Add the egg yolks to the rice mixture. Whisk the whites in a scrupulously clean bowl until they form stiff peaks. Gently fold the whites into the rice mixture a tablespoon at a time.

Place the 100 g of sugar in a heavy-based saucepan and cook on a high heat, without stirring, until it forms a rich amber caramel. Pour this into the bottom of each ramekin and then fill the ramekins with the rice mixture.

Place the ramekins in a roasting tin and fill the tin three-quarters of the way up with boiling water. Bake for 20 minutes. Remove from the oven, cool for 2 minutes and then carefully run a knife along the inside of the ramekin. Turn out onto dishes.

To make the compote, bring a pot of water to the boil. Score the top of each peach with a knife and plunge into the water. After 15 seconds, remove the peaches from the boiling water and plunge into a bowl of cold water. Peel the peaches, cut in half and remove the stone. Place the honey, sugar and water in a saucepan. Split the vanilla pod lengthwise and scrape out the seeds into the saucepan. Add the pod and simmer until the sugar has dissolved, about 5 minutes.

Cut each peach half in half and add to the sugar syrup with the lemon juice and limoncello. Cover with greaseproof paper and simmer until the peaches are soft – this will depend on ripeness, but should take about 10 minutes. Remove the peaches, bring the syrup to the boil and reduce by half. Place the peaches in a container and cover with the syrup. This will keep covered in the fridge for up to a week. Serve alongside the candied rice puddings.

june

june

There's something very romantic and nostalgic about the notion of a picnic. Unfortunately, the reality is often a washed-out affair with curled-up sandwiches, warm wine and frayed tempers. I can't guarantee the weather, but the food in this chapter won't let you down.

When planning a picnic, make sure you have the facilities to keep your food and drinks cold. Use cool bags or tiffin boxes (individual boxes that are held within an insulated container) to ensure the food is safely held at a constant temperature. I also like to add a box of ice to the cool bag to use for drinks and to provide extra coolness.

A whole roasted stuffed chicken is a great dish for sharing – rip it apart and dip each piece into a hot harissa dressing. The salads in this chapter would be equally good with hot roast chicken, served in the comfort of your kitchen, as they are in a picnic.

If your natural inclination on a day out like this is sandwiches, then make the New Orleans-style muffaletta – it's like a deli counter in a loaf!

For vegetarians, there are lovely goat's cheese, sweet potato and pecan nut pies and for the fish eaters, a miso and sesame-crusted tuna with a runner bean salad (like an Oriental twist on the classic salade Niçoise).

I've also included two of my favourite puds – custardy white chocolate and mascarpone tartlets and a Bananas Foster cream pie.

Make the food for the picnic anyway and if it rains (as would be typical of our weather), light the fire and enjoy the feast in the comfort of your own home – not a bee sting in sight!

moroccan-spiced stuffed chicken with harissa sauce

Serves 4

My favourite way of eating roast chicken is when it's cold. Spice and stuff the chicken before roasting and you have a perfect al fresco dish for a picnic or just outside with friends. I'd serve this with crusty bread, mixed salad leaves and a bottle or two of chilled Beaujolais.

Harissa is traditionally a fiery spiced chilli dip, but I substitute roast red pepper for some of the chilli and whisk in a little sour cream to cool the whole thing down. This is also excellent with oily fish or as a dip for homemade chips.

Moroccan-spiced chicken:
1 x 2 kg chicken
2 tablespoons olive oil
25 g butter
1 medium onion, peeled and finely chopped
2 cloves garlic, chopped finely
1 teaspoon chopped fresh red chilli
6 cardamom pods
1 teaspoon ground coriander
1 teaspoon turmeric
½ teaspoon ground cumin
50 g pistachio nuts, shelled and finely chopped
75 g dried apricots, chopped
handful each of fresh coriander and mint, chopped
zest and juice of 1 lemon
100 g breadcrumbs
salt and pepper

Rub for chicken:
2 tablespoons olive oil
1 teaspoon smoked paprika powder
1 teaspoon ground coriander
½ teaspoon turmeric
1 teaspoon salt

Harissa dressing:
2 red peppers
1 large red chilli pepper
salt
1 teaspoon ground coriander
1 teaspoon ground cumin
3 cloves roast garlic (see p. 8)
zest and juice of 1 lemon
100 ml olive oil
100 ml sour cream
1 tablespoon chopped fresh mint leaves
handful fresh chopped coriander
salt and pepper

To make the chicken, melt the oil and butter in a saucepan over medium heat. Add the onion, garlic and chilli, season well and cook for 5 minutes. Split the cardamom pods, remove the black seeds and bash them with a rolling pin or in a mortar and pestle until fine. Add the cardamom, ground coriander, turmeric and cumin to the onion mixture and cook for 1 minute to release the flavours. Add the pistachios and apricots and cook for 2 minutes. Remove from the heat and add the fresh herbs, lemon zest and juice and breadcrumbs. Mix well and check the seasoning.

To make the rub, simply mix all the ingredients together.

Preheat the oven to 180°C. Stuff the chicken by loosening the skin over the breasts and filling the gap with stuffing. Rub the flavoured oil over the outside of the chicken. If you have a cooking pot with a lid (like a Le Creuset), place the chicken in this and cover. Alternatively, place the chicken in a roasting tin and cover with foil. Bake for 2 hours. Remove the foil, turn the heat up to 210°C and cook the chicken until the skin crisps and is golden, about another 20 minutes. To check if the chicken is ready, pierce the drumstick: if the juices run clear, the chicken is cooked.

To make the harissa, preheat the oven to 200°C. Brush the red peppers and chilli with oil and season with salt. Place on a roasting tray and cook until scorched and blackened – about 10 minutes for the chilli, 20 minutes for the red pepper. Place in a plastic bag and leave for 5 minutes to sweat and make the skin easier to remove. Peel and deseed the peppers and chilli and place in the jug of a liquidiser.

Dry fry the spices in a frying pan until they start to release their fragrance, about 30 seconds. Add to the roasted chilli and peppers and blend with the remaining ingredients to a smooth paste. Check the seasoning.

grilled sweet potato, pancetta and red onion salad

Serves 4

Sweet potatoes really suit being chargrilled (or barbecued) – the hot smokiness counterbalances the intense sweetness of the vegetable. Likewise, slightly salty pancetta cuts through the sweetness and crisp red onions give the whole dish a zingy crunch.

Salad:
2 large sweet potatoes
olive oil
salt and pepper
10 rashers of smoked pancetta
2 medium red onions, peeled and finely sliced

Salpicon dressing:
2 teaspoons cumin seeds
4 scallions, finely chopped
2 cloves roast garlic (see p. 8)
1 tablespoon Dijon mustard
juice of 1 lemon
2 tablespoons red wine vinegar
100 ml extra virgin olive oil
salt and pepper

To make the salad, preheat the oven to 200°C. Scrub the sweet potatoes and dry them, then slice into 1 cm thick rounds. Brush a baking sheet with oil and place the sweet potatoes on top. Brush the top of the potatoes with oil and lightly sprinkle with salt and pepper. Cover with foil and bake for 25 minutes, or until the potatoes are soft. Set aside.

Heat a grill pan, and when smoking hot, cook the pancetta until crisp and golden. Drain off some of the oil but use some to cook the potatoes. Add the sweet potato slices to the pan and cook for about 20 seconds on each side, until scorched. Place on a platter, crumble the pancetta on top and scatter over the onions.

To make the dressing, toast the cumin seeds in a dry pan until they start to pop, about 30 seconds. Place in a bowl and add the other ingredients, except the olive oil and seasoning. Whisk together and then add the olive oil in a steady stream, whisking as you go. Check the seasoning.

Drizzle the salpicon dressing all over the sweet potatoes and leave for at least 30 minutes before serving to allow the dressing to permeate through.

couscous salad with grilled courgettes, pine nuts, mint and avocado

Serves 4

Toasting couscous in butter and oil before adding the stock gives the finished dish a lovely nuttiness. The courgettes and pine nuts give crunch to the dish and the avocado adds a fresh zinginess. Serve this salad with salmon, chicken or even grilled steaks.

3 tablespoons olive oil
25 g butter
200 g couscous
400 ml hot chicken or vegetable stock (see p. 11)
2 courgettes
1 teaspoon chilli powder
juice of 2 limes
1 teaspoon caster sugar
2 ripe avocadoes
50 ml extra virgin oil or avocado oil
handful fresh mint leaves, chopped
1 red onion, finely chopped
2 scallions, finely chopped
50 g pine nuts
salt and pepper

Heat 1 tablespoon of the olive oil and the butter in a large saucepan and when foaming, add the couscous. Cook until the couscous starts to colour, about 1 minute. Add the hot stock and cover with cling film or a lid and set aside.

Heat a grill pan or barbecue until smoking hot. Slice the courgettes into rings about ½ cm thick. Mix 2 tablespoons of oil with the chilli powder and brush over the courgettes. Cook on the griddle, seasoning with salt as you cook. Place in a bowl.

Place the lime juice in a separate bowl with the caster sugar. Cut the avocado in half, remove the stone and peel. Cut into 1 cm dice and toss in the lime juice. Add the extra virgin olive oil, mint, onion, scallions and season to taste. Toast the pine nuts in a dry pan until golden, about 1 minute.

Remove the cling film or lid from the couscous after 5 minutes and fluff up with a fork. Cool completely, then add the avocado mixture, cooked courgettes, pine nuts and mix together. Check the seasoning.

orzo pasta with asparagus and creamy gremolata dressing

Serves 4

Orzo is rice-shaped pasta that's now widely available. It's ideal for salads, as you get the best of both worlds – a rice/pasta salad rolled into one. Now is the time of year to eat local asparagus. Lightly blanching it and then finishing on a barbecue or chargrill gives it a new dimension. Gremolata is a simple paste of garlic, parsley and lemon that is traditionally served with braised veal shank (osso bucco). Mixed into a creamy dressing, it makes all the other ingredients sing. Gremolata is also great with roast chicken or pork.

Pasta:
250 g orzo pasta
1 teaspoon salt
1 bunch asparagus, each stem snapped where
  it naturally breaks
2 tablespoons olive oil

Creamy gremolata dressing:
zest and juice of 2 lemons
65 g flat leaf parsley leaves
4 cloves roast garlic (see p. 8)
1 teaspoon caster sugar
100 ml crème fraîche
100 ml extra virgin olive oil
salt and pepper

To make the pasta, bring a large saucepan of water to the boil. Add the orzo and salt. Cook the orzo according to the manufacturer's instructions. One minute before the orzo is cooked, add the asparagus.

Drain the pasta and asparagus in a colander and run cold water over them until they're cool. Remove the asparagus and dry on kitchen paper, then toss in 1 tablespoon of the olive oil. Add the other tablespoon of oil to the pasta and toss thoroughly to prevent sticking. Transfer to a bowl.

Heat a grill pan until smoking hot and grill the asparagus until it has marks on the side. Cut each spear into 4 pieces and add to the pasta.

To make the gremolata, blend all the ingredients in a food processor and season to taste. Toss into the orzo and asparagus.

muffaletta sandwich

Serves 4

This is a classic sandwich from New Orleans that is essentially the deli counter packed into a cob loaf. It's ideal for a picnic, as everything is tightly packed together, and is a meal in itself.

1 large round cob or country loaf
2 tablespoons good-quality mayonnaise
50 g green olives, finely chopped
10 sunblush tomatoes
1 punnet cherry plum tomatoes, halved
6 slices pastrami
12 slices salami
100 g grated Gruyère cheese
2 red onions, finely sliced
4 gherkins, finely chopped
handful fresh chopped flat leaf parsley
2 tablespoons extra virgin olive oil
salt and pepper

Cut the loaf in half through the circumference. Spread each half with the mayonnaise and place the bottom half on a large sheet of greaseproof paper. Sprinkle the olives and sunblush tomatoes on top. Scatter over the cherry plum tomatoes and season with salt and pepper. Arrange the pastrami and salami on top of the tomatoes and sprinkle with the cheese. Add the onions, gherkins and parsley and drizzle over the oil and season to taste. Place the other half of the loaf on top. Wrap up in the greaseproof paper like a parcel and weigh the whole thing down with two or three plates. Leave for 20 minutes, remove the plates and paper and slice into 6 or 8 wedges.

miso and sesame seed-crusted tuna

Serves 4

Miso is a Japanese soy bean paste that's available in some supermarkets and Asian shops. It's terrific in this dish, as it has a delicious salty taste, but also helps the sesame seeds to adhere to the tuna. A squeeze of honey will help cut through the saltiness and give the finish a sugary glow. Black sesame seeds are available in Asian shops, but just use regular white ones if you can't get black.

Serve this with the runner bean, macadamia nut and lemongrass salad on p. 91, though the tuna loin would also work well with the cucumber pickle on p. 99.

1 tablespoon miso paste
1 teaspoon honey
1 teaspoon rice wine vinegar
1 kg tuna loin
1 tablespoon white sesame seeds
1 tablespoon black sesame seeds
1 tablespoon vegetable oil

Mix the miso, honey and vinegar to a paste and brush all over the tuna.

Take a sheet of cling film and sprinkle the seeds in the middle, mixing them up well. Roll the tuna all over the seeds, making sure it's evenly coated. Wrap tightly in the cling film and chill for 1 hour.

Heat the oil in a large frying pan until smoking hot, then carefully add the tuna. Move the tuna around the pan until all sides are seared. Allow to rest, then slice with a sharp knife and arrange around a platter with a space in the middle for the bean salad on p. 91.

runner bean, macadamia nut and lemongrass salad

Serves 4

Local runner beans are at their sprightly best now and are perfect for blanching and tossing immediately into a zippy dressing. Macadamia nuts have a natural creaminess about them without being too 'claggy'.

350 g runner beans
75 g macadamia nuts, roughly chopped
100 ml avocado oil
zest and juice of 1 lime
pinch sugar
1 shallot, peeled and finely chopped
salt and pepper
2 stalks lemongrass
4 scallions
handful chopped fresh coriander

Top and tail the runner beans, then slice into 3 cm pieces on the bias. Bring a pot of salted water to the boil.

Toast the macadamia nuts in a dry pan until golden, about 1 minute. Place half the nuts in a blender with the avocado oil, lime zest and juice, sugar and shallot. Blend to a smooth dressing and season to taste.

Top and tail the lemongrass and remove any tough outer leaves. Chop as finely as you can and add to the dressing. Coarsely grate the remaining nuts and finely slice the scallions on the bias.

Plunge the runner beans into the boiling water and cook for 2 minutes. Drain and place in a bowl. Add the dressing while still hot and mix well. Add the scallions and coriander. Scatter over the grated macadamias.

sweet potato pies with goat's cheese

Serves 4

These vegetarian pies are a real crowd pleaser. I first made them on the *Saturday Magazine* show on BBC Radio Ulster for Vegetarian Week and was enthusiastically shocked at how the die-hard carnivores wolfed them down. If you don't like goat's cheese, substitute a sharp cheddar, feta, Taleggio or your own favourite.

Pecan nut pastry:
225 g plain flour
50 g pecan nuts
½ teaspoon salt
75 g butter, chilled and cut into ½ cm cubes
1 medium egg
1 tablespoon water

Filling:
2 tablespoons olive oil
300 g peeled sweet potato, cut into 1 cm dice
½ medium red onion, finely chopped
1 clove garlic, chopped
1 tablespoon sage, rosemary and thyme leaves
125 g goat's cheese (if using a hard variety, coarsely grate it)
salt and pepper
1 egg yolk + 1 tablespoon of water, mixed together

To make the pastry, blend the flour, pecan nuts and salt to a fine powder in a food processor. Add the butter and process until it resembles fine breadcrumbs. Add the egg and water and process until the mixture comes together. Wrap in cling film and chill.

To make the filling, preheat the oven to 200°C. Heat 1 tablespoon of the oil in a frying pan and, when hot, add the sweet potatoes. Cook for 1 minute, stirring as you go. Season with salt and pepper, then place in a roasting tin and transfer to the preheated oven. Bake for about 10 minutes, or until the sweet potatoes are soft. Reduce the heat to 180°C.

Heat the remaining oil in a saucepan and add the onion and garlic. Cook until soft, then add the herbs, cooking for a further 1 minute. Season and add this to the sweet potatoes. Allow to cool, then add the goat's cheese.

Divide the pastry into 8 pieces and roll each one into a ball. Roll each ball out into a round about 8 cm in diameter. You can trim round the edges or go for a rustic look. Brush the edges with the egg yolk and water mixture. Place a dollop of the sweet potato mix in the middle and fold the pastry over into a semi-circle, sealing the edges well. Repeat with the remaining dough and sweet potato mix.

Place the pies on a tray lined with non-stick parchment paper. Brush each with the egg yolk. Chill until ready to use, then bake in an oven preheated to 180°C until golden brown, about 20 minutes.

white chocolate and mascarpone tarts with fresh berries

Makes 12 tarts

Individual custard tarts are a perfect picnic dish – they are easy to eat and taste fabulous. Adding white chocolate and mascarpone gives these a cheesecake feel. They are also the perfect vehicle for fresh local berries, tossed here in a little fruit liqueur to give them a bit of oomph.

6 large egg yolks
100 g caster sugar
2 tablespoons cornflour
100 ml double cream
200 ml whole milk
1 vanilla pod
50 g good-quality white chocolate, chopped
100 g mascarpone cheese
300 g ready rolled puff pastry
250 g mixed berries (raspberries, strawberries, tayberries and loganberries are all good)
1 tablespoon raspberry or strawberry liqueur

Place the egg yolks, sugar and cornflour in a heavy-based saucepan and whisk together. Whisk in the cream and milk. Split the vanilla pod and scrape the seeds into the pan with the pod. Place the saucepan on a medium heat and stir constantly until the mixture thickens and is hot. Remove from the heat, remove the vanilla pod and stir in the chopped chocolate until it's melted. Transfer the mix to a bowl and cover the surface with cling film to prevent a skin forming. Leave to cool. When cool, whisk in the mascarpone.

Preheat the oven to 180°C. Either lightly grease a 12-hole muffin tin or grease individual metal rings.

Lay out the pastry and cut into 12 pieces. Roll each piece into a circle approximately 12 cm across. Press into the muffin tins or metal rings and cut around the pastry to trim. Spoon the cold custard mix into the pastry cups, filling them ¾ full, and bake for 20 to 25 minutes, or until the pastry and custard are golden. Leave to rest in the tin for 10 minutes, then transfer to a wire rack to cool. The custard will sink a little, to allow room for the berries.

Mix the berries with the liqueur and spoon over the tarts when ready to serve.

dark chocolate brownie and Bananas Foster cream pie

Serves 4

This New Orleans-inspired cream pie is normally made with a pastry base and pastry cream, but this version is less complicated and a lot tastier. Bananas Foster are bananas flamed with rum and cinnamon.

Dark chocolate brownie base:
225 g dark chocolate, chopped into 1 cm chunks
175 g butter, chopped into 1 cm chunks
3 large eggs
125 g muscovado sugar
125 g caster sugar
100 g plain flour

Bananas Foster cream:
25 g butter
1 tablespoon Demerara sugar
2 large bananas, peeled and chopped
pinch cinnamon
juice of ½ lemon
good dash golden rum
500 ml double cream
1 tablespoon icing sugar
grated dark chocolate, to decorate (optional)

To make the brownie base, preheat the oven to 180°C. Place the chocolate and butter in a heatproof bowl over a pot of very gently simmering water to melt. Ensure that the bottom of the bowl isn't touching the water.

Meanwhile, whisk the eggs and sugars together until pale and thick and the whisk leaves tracks in the mixture. Whisk in the melted chocolate mixture until it's fully incorporated. Sift and fold in the flour.

Butter and line a 10-inch round cake tin with non-stick parchment paper. Pour the brownie batter into the cake and bake for about 25 minutes. The brownie should be slightly wobbly and not too firm to the touch.

Cool the brownie slightly, then carefully place on a large plate or cake stand. Cover and set aside – do not put in the fridge, as it will go hard.

To make the Bananas Foster cream, heat the butter in a large frying pan until foaming. Add the sugar and bananas. Stir until the sugar has dissolved and the bananas are golden, about 2 minutes. Add the cinnamon, cook for 20 seconds and add the lemon and rum – be careful if the rum flames. Cool.

Whip the cream to soft peaks, then fold in the Bananas Foster and icing sugar. Cover and chill until ready to serve the cake.

To serve, spread the Bananas Foster cream over the brownie. You could decorate with grated dark chocolate if you wish. Serve immediately.

a kitchen year

july

july

Eating with friends and family should be a fun, relaxing experience. But how often does entertaining become a joyless chore? I think there are few things worse than the cook for the evening being stuck in the kitchen while everyone else is enjoying themselves. For this reason, July is a perfect time to pay back all those people you owe an invitation! This is the time of year to serve platters of cold food for everyone to help themselves.

There's such an abundance of beautiful produce around this month – hothouse cucumbers, wild salmon, lobsters, sweetcorn, strawberries, gooseberries and elderflower.

I've included my recipe for cured salmon in which you're actually 'cooking' the salmon in salt and sugar, which draws out the moisture and leaves you with a soft-textured fish. Crunchy cucumber pickles add a tangy flavour and texture contrast to the salmon.

If you've never tried cooking a lobster, now is the time. For me, there is nothing as quintessentially summer as a lobster. I had lobster grilled on a barbecue in Martha's Vineyard in Massachusetts, served with buttery corn, and it was one of the most amazing things I've ever tasted. Here, the lobster's boiled and served with a roast corn dressing which is just as delicious (mightn't taste as good in Ballymuck, though!).

If you're lucky enough to have a good butcher (and you should be, because Ireland is full of them), then you'll know the joys of cold roast sirloin. Rare cold roast beef (or cook it to your liking) is just begging to be served with sticky red onion jam and a smoky, creamy dressing.

And summer wouldn't be summer without a trifle. I'm a firm believer in jelly in a trifle and strawberries suspended in a sparkling wine jelly will always do it for me. Some soft ripe peaches will liven up the regular custard.

Gooseberries are starting to appear now. My freezer is always full of summer gooseberries – nothing beats a gooseberry fool in November. Elderflowers and gooseberries make great partners, and what better way to combine them than in a creamy almond tart?

If you've ever considered making your own wine, start now with elderflower champagne. The satisfaction of making your own is overwhelming! And bottle those local strawberries in a vodka. Imagine that cocktail on Christmas morning!

fennel-cured salmon

Serves 4

I have a wee bit of an obsession with curing and smoking food. My brother, David, a keen fisherman, shares this condition and we were constantly wasting a lot of his treasured, freshly caught wild salmon in the search for the perfect cure. Ironically, it was with a piece of supermarket bought, farmed salmon that I finally cracked the perfect cure. Leave out the fennel and chilli if you want a simpler version.

Serve this with the cucumber pickle on p. 99.

1 dessertspoon fennel seeds
100 g Demerara sugar
100 g caster sugar
75 g coarse sea salt
2 shallots, peeled and finely chopped
1 teaspoon finely chopped green chilli
1 kg piece salmon fillet

Toast the fennel seeds in a dry pan until they start to pop, about 30 seconds. Cool the seeds and either grind them in a mortar and pestle or in a coffee grinder. Mix the ground seeds with the sugars, salt, chopped shallots and chilli.

Line the bottom of a roasting dish or large tin with cling film. Sprinkle over about a third of the sugar mix and place the salmon in the middle of the mixture. Gather up all the mix to pack around the salmon. Sprinkle over the remaining sugar mix, pressing it in as tightly round the salmon as possible. Take another sheet of cling film and cover the salmon. Now take a tray or plate that will fit on top of the salmon and weight it down – I do this with whatever tins I have in the cupboard or beer cans from the fridge. Refrigerate for 48 hours. Remove all the weights after this time – the sugar and salt mix should now be a liquid that has cured the salmon. Wash the salmon in cold water for a couple of minutes, then pat dry with kitchen paper. Wrap in greaseproof until ready to use. This will keep for a week in the fridge. Slice as thinly as you can.

cucumber pickle

Makes approximately 500 g pickle

Cucumber pickle is one of those simple things that always gets an awesome reaction. It's great with most fish, cured meats and salamis and will keep in the fridge for up to a week.

1 tablespoon yellow mustard seeds
1 teaspoon black onion seeds (nigella seeds)
½ teaspoon turmeric
200 ml white wine vinegar
150 g caster sugar
1 teaspoon salt
2 cucumbers
1 red onion, finely sliced

Toast the mustard and nigella seeds in a dry saucepan until they pop, about 30 seconds. Add the turmeric, give it a quick stir and then add the vinegar – don't look into the pan, as the vinegar will sting your eyes. Lower the heat and add the sugar and salt and simmer gently until the sugar dissolves.

Peel the cucumbers and slice down through the middle, lengthwise. Scoop out the seeds with a teaspoon or melon baller. Slice the cucumber thinly, preferably on the bias for a nice effect. Mix the cucumber and red onion together and add to the cool sugar and vinegar solution. Stir and leave to marinate in the fridge for 1 hour.

lobster with creamy roasted corn dressing

Serves 4

Unfortunately, there is only one way of buying lobsters – live! According to animal welfare associations, to kill them humanely, you need to leave them in the freezer for 10 minutes (they apparently fall into a catatonic state) and then plunge them into boiling, salted water. Make sure there's plenty of water in the pot to cover the lobster. After the water comes back to the boil, lower the heat, put the lid on and simmer – a 550 g lobster will take 12 minutes at this stage, a 700 g to 900 g one will take 15 to 18 minutes and a lobster over a kilo will take 20 to 25 minutes.

After cooking, pull the claws from the lobster and crack them with a rolling pin. Pull out the meat with either specialised lobster skewers or with a teaspoon handle. Press the main body of the lobster together and then pull back the 'legs' – the body piece of meat should come out easily.

1 x 550 g lobster per person

Creamy roasted corn dressing:
1 red chilli
2 tablespoons oil, plus a little extra
2 ears corn, boiled in salted water for 5
 minutes
2 shallots, finely chopped
2 cloves garlic, finely chopped
100 ml sour cream
100 ml mayonnaise
juice of 1 lime
salt and pepper

Arrange the lobster on a plate of leaves and serve with the roast corn dressing. Alternatively, just serve warm with some melted butter, lemon wedges and chips. You'll need one 550 g lobster per person (they're not cheap, so save them for special occasions).

Another way of cooking lobster is to boil them for 2 minutes less than the allocated time. Split the whole lobster with a hardy, sharp knife right through the head and down through the middle of the body. Brush with a little oil and then warm through on the barbecue, shell side down, and cook for 30 seconds on the flesh side. You'll get that gorgeous smell of warm shell that's like a really hot beach. Also, your guests will do all the work to remove the meat themselves! Everyone's a winner.

To make the dressing, brush the chilli with a little oil and roast in a 200°C oven for 10 minutes. Peel and deseed the chilli, chop and place in a bowl. Heat 1 tablespoon of oil in a frying pan until smoking. Add the corn and cook until golden on all sides. Allow to cool, then shuck the niblets from the corn by slicing them off with a sharp knife.

Heat another tablespoon of oil in a saucepan and add the shallots and garlic. Cook until golden. Remove from the heat and cool slightly. Add the chilli, sour cream, mayonnaise, lime juice and roasted corn. Blend the mixture to a smooth sauce and check for seasoning.

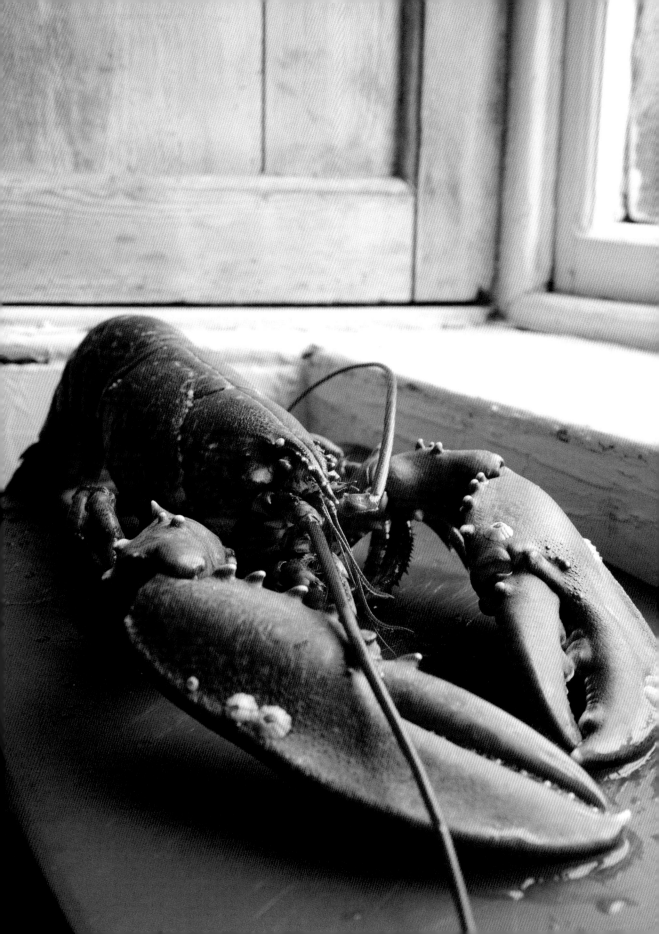

spiced sirloin of beef

Serves 4

The key to serving roast sirloin cold is to ensure you have a good piece of meat to start with. Make friends with your butcher and ask him to hang meat for you for up to 28 days, which will make all the difference.

Serve this with red onion jam and triple smoked chilli sour cream dressing (p. 104).

1 tablespoon coriander seeds
1 teaspoon cumin seeds
2 teaspoons black peppercorns
2 teaspoons chopped, deseeded red chilli
2 kg piece of whole sirloin, fat removed
1 teaspoon sea salt
2 tablespoons olive oil

Grind the seeds and peppercorns in a mortar and pestle or coffee grinder. Mix in the chopped chilli. Take a sheet of cling film and sprinkle the mixture all over it. Roll the sirloin all round to coat evenly with the spice mixture and then wrap tightly in the cling film. Chill for at least 1 hour and up to 6. Remove the meat from the fridge 30 minutes prior to cooking.

Preheat the oven to 200°C and remove the cling film. Season well all over with the salt. Heat the oil in a large frying pan until smoking hot and cook the sirloin for about 30 seconds on each side, being careful not to burn the spices. Place in a roasting tray and cover with foil. Bake for 15 minutes for rare meat. Rest for 10 minutes, then slice thinly.

red onion jam

Makes 250 g

Red onions have a natural sweetness that makes them ideal for turning into a sticky jam made zingy with red wine and red wine vinegar. The sweet and sour combination is delicious with roast meats, especially beef. The jam has an intense, luxurious, deep red appearance that makes beef look even more appetising.

1 tablespoon olive oil
2 large red onions, peeled and finely sliced
2 cloves garlic, crushed
½ teaspoon salt
200 ml red wine
50 ml red wine vinegar
100 g Demerara sugar

Heat the oil in large saucepan and add the onions, garlic and salt. Cook on a low heat for 10 minutes, or until the onions start to soften. Add the red wine, red wine vinegar and sugar and simmer until the mixture is thick and syrupy, about 30 minutes. Check the seasoning again. Cool and store in a jam jar or airtight container for up to a week.

smoked chilli sour cream dressing

Makes 300 ml

I love chillies as they are, but smoked, they are sublime. This recipe involves combining three types of smoked chilli – sultry, dried chipotle from Mexico, a zingy fresh smoked chilli and sweet smoked paprika powder from Spain. You could simply use one type of smoked chilli, but the flavours here balance really well.

1 chipotle chilli
1 fresh smoked red chilli
1 teaspoon sweet smoked paprika
200 ml sour cream
100 ml extra virgin olive oil
1 teaspoon mustard
juice of 1 lime
2 cloves roast garlic (see p. 8)
2 shallots, chopped

Soak the chipotle chilli in hot water for 20 minutes. Remove the seeds for a slightly cooler version or leave them in if you like it hot.

To make the dressing, simply blend all the ingredients together.

This will keep in the fridge for up to 1 week.

polenta scones with olives, Parmesan and sunblush tomatoes

Serves 4

Some polenta in a traditional scone mix will give it a lovely hint of crunch. Olives, Parmesan and sunblush tomatoes give the finished scones a brilliant savouriness and all the benefit of warm baked bread with none of the effort of kneading or proving.

300 g plain flour
1 heaped teaspoon baking soda
200 g polenta
½ teaspoon baking powder
1 teaspoon salt
75 g chilled butter
6 sunblush tomatoes, chopped
6 good-quality black olives, chopped
1 teaspoon chopped fresh rosemary leaves
25 g finely grated fresh Parmesan
3 medium eggs
50 ml buttermilk
1 egg yolk

Preheat the oven to 200°C.

Sift the flour, baking soda, polenta, baking powder and salt into a baking bowl. Rub in the butter until the mixture resembles fine breadcrumbs. Add the tomatoes, olives, rosemary and Parmesan and mix well.

In a separate bowl, whisk the eggs lightly with the buttermilk. Make a well in the centre of the dry ingredients and add the wet ingredients. Mix well to a dough and turn out onto a floured surface.

Knead the mix lightly into a ball and then roll out to a thickness of 2 cm. Cut into the desired sizes and shapes and place on a lightly floured baking tray. Mix the remaining egg yolk with 1 teaspoon of water and brush over the top of the scones. Bake until golden brown – this will take approximately 15 minutes, but will depend on the size of the scones. Turn one upside down and if it sounds hollow when tapped, it's ready. Cool on a wire rack and serve as soon as possible, split and spread with butter.

peach and strawberry trifle

Serves 4

Trifle is a timeless classic dish that transcends the seasons. This version is summer in a bowl, packed with strawberries, peaches and lemon pound cake. But it's equally suitable for winter feasting – would Christmas be the same without a trifle beside the plum pudding?

I belong to the untrendy camp of people who believe a trifle isn't the same without jelly, and I'm not changing for any fashion!

You could always substitute a bought Madeira sponge for the lemon almond pound cake. The pound cake is also good scattered with fresh strawberries and whipped cream.

Lemon almond pound cake:
150 g butter, at room temperature
150 g caster sugar
3 medium eggs
150 g ground almonds
250 g self-raising flour
zest of 2 lemons (reserve juice for the jelly)

Strawberry jelly:
400 ml sparkling dry white or rosé wine
150 g caster sugar
juice from lemons above
1 vanilla pod
500 g strawberries, hulls removed and
  quartered
5 gelatine leaves

Roast peach and honey custard:
2 ripe peaches
1 tablespoon honey
500 ml whole milk
1 vanilla pod
5 large egg yolks
50 g caster sugar
25 g cornflour
100 g mascarpone cheese

500 ml whipping cream
whole strawberries, to decorate
mint leaves, to decorate

To make the pound cake, preheat the oven to 170°C and lightly butter a loaf tin.

Beat the butter and sugar until pale and fluffy. Beat in the eggs one at a time until incorporated. Fold in the almonds and then sift in the flour. Fold together with the lemon zest.

Bake for 30 minutes, or until an inserted skewer comes out clean.

Allow the cake to cool, then cut the pound cake in half. Freeze one half or just eat it. Cut off the crust from the remaining half. Cut into 2 cm cubes and place in the bottom of a large glass bowl.

To make the strawberry jelly, place the wine, sugar and lemon juice in a saucepan. Split the vanilla pod, scrape the seeds into the pan and add the pod. Simmer until the sugar has dissolved, about 2 minutes. Meanwhile, soak the gelatine leaves in cold water for 5 minutes. Remove the pod from the mixture and add the gelatine and half the strawberries, setting aside the other half to decorate the dish later. Pour the jelly onto the sponge, cool and refrigerate to set.

To make the custard, bring a pot of water to the boil. Score the top of the peaches with a knife and plunge into the boiling water. Count to 10 and then place in a bowl of iced water. Peel the peaches, cut in half and remove the stones, then cut the peaches into 2 cm dice. Heat a large frying pan and when smoking hot, add the peaches. Cook for 1 minute, stirring all the time, until they start to caramelise slightly. Add the honey, then place in a bowl to cool.

Place the milk in a saucepan. Split the vanilla pod lengthwise and scrape the seeds into the milk. Place the milk on a low heat. Whisk the egg yolks, sugar and cornflour to a smooth paste. Pour over the hot milk and whisk well. Return to the saucepan and stir until the mixture thickens. When it does thicken, pour into a bowl and cover the surface with cling film. Allow to cool completely. When cool, remove the vanilla pod, whisk in the mascarpone and then fold in the peaches. Pour the custard over the set jelly and return to the fridge.

To finish the trifle, whisk the whipping cream to soft peaks. If you wish, sweeten the cream with 1 tablespoon of icing sugar. Fold the remaining strawberries into the cream. Spread over the custard and serve. Decorate with whole strawberries and mint leaves.

lorna's elderflower champagne

Serves 4

Lorna is a classroom assistant in one of the colleges I teach in and nobody makes a better elderflower champagne than she does. This is a great way of using the free elderflowers that are in abundance all over the countryside at this time of year. The result is completely delicious and potent. This drink is beautiful on its own or poured over fresh local strawberries. Rustic chic!

1 pint glass packed with elderflowers (just the flowers – no green stalks)
juice and rind of 1 lemon
1 dessertspoon cider vinegar
750 g granulated sugar
700 ml water

Pour boiled water into a large bowl and then tip out to sterilise the bowl. Place the elderflowers, lemon juice, rind and cider vinegar into the bowl, mix around and cover with a clean tea towel. Leave for a couple of days to ferment the flowers, giving them the odd stir.

When the liquid in the bowl is yellow, strain into a clean jug. Sterilise a demijohn by pouring in boiling water and then pouring it out. Pour in the strained elderflower liquid.

Boil the sugar and water together until the sugar has dissolved. Cool this and add to the demijohn. Airlock the demijohn and leave in a warm place for 6 weeks to ferment.

After 6 weeks, decant the elderflower 'wine' into bottles with a good firm screw top. Decant to three-quarters of the way up the bottle and add a dessertspoon of sugar. Place the top on tightly and leave for a week before opening. Chill before serving.

strawberry sorbet with strawberry and vanilla vodka

Serves 4

Strawberries are gorgeous at the moment, and to preserve their loveliness for dark winter nights, I make them into a cordial and combine that with vodka and vanilla. Enjoy the strawberry sorbet now and keep some of the vodka in the fridge for Christmas.

Strawberry sorbet:
juice and zest of 1 lemon
175 g caster sugar
250 ml water
1 tablespoon liquid glucose
350 g strawberries, washed and hulled

Strawberry and vanilla vodka:
500 g strawberries, washed and green tops removed
900 g caster sugar
2 lemons
500 ml water
1 vanilla pod
500 ml vodka

To make the sorbet, place the lemon zest, juice, sugar, water and glucose in a saucepan and simmer until all the sugar has dissolved. Cool.

Blend the strawberries with the sugar syrup to a smooth purée, then pass through a sieve. Churn in an ice cream maker if you have one. If not, pour the mixture into a plastic tray, place in the freezer and churn up with a fork after 30 minutes. Repeat this every half hour to stop ice crystals forming.

To make the strawberry vodka, crush the strawberries and sugar together until mashed to a pulp. Chop the lemons up and place in a saucepan with the water. Split the vanilla pod, scrape the seeds into the saucepan and add the pod. Simmer for 10 minutes, then add the strawberry mixture. Simmer for a further 20 minutes. Allow to stand for 2 hours, then strain the liquid through a fine sieve. Bring to the boil again in a clean saucepan and pass the hot mix through a coffee filter. Cool. Mix in the vodka and pour into sterilised bottles.

To serve, scoop the sorbet into chilled martini or wine glasses and drizzle over a good dash of the vodka.

gooseberry and elderflower frangipane tart

Serves 4

Gooseberries and elderflowers are one of those serendipitous seasonal flavour combinations that are classic. Lightly poached gooseberries infused with some elderflowers are glorious on their own served with some cream. Suspend the gooseberries in a tart of classic frangipane (a light almond, egg and butter mixture) and you have something ethereal. You could serve this with cream or ice cream, but using up the liquid from cooking the gooseberries to make a lemon and almond cream finishes the whole thing off fantastically.

Shortcrust pastry:
225 g plain flour
150 g butter
75 g caster sugar
1 egg yolk
1 tablespoon ice cold water

Gooseberry and elderflower compote:
4 elderflower heads
250 g gooseberries
75 g sugar

Frangipane:
125 g butter at room temperature
125 g caster sugar
2 medium eggs
100 g ground almonds
60 g plain flour

Almond cream:
reserved gooseberry cooking liquid from
  gooseberry compote
zest and juice of 1 lemon
50 g nibbed almonds
200 ml double cream

To make the pastry, rub the flour and butter together (you could do this in a food processor) until the mixture resembles fine breadcrumbs. Add the sugar and mix well. Mix the egg yolk with the water and use this to form a dough with the flour mixture. Wrap in cling film and chill for 30 minutes.

To make the compote, pick the elderflowers, wrap in a piece of muslin and tie with a piece of string. Place the gooseberries and sugar in a non-reactive saucepan and simmer. Poke the muslin bag into the middle. Cook gently until the gooseberries are soft, about 10 minutes. Cool, then strain off the liquid and set aside.

To make the frangipane, beat the butter and sugar until pale and fluffy. Add the eggs one at a time, beating between each addition. Sift the almonds and flour and fold into the butter mixture.

To make the almond cream, boil the gooseberry liquid, lemon zest and juice until thick and syrupy. Cool.

Toast the almonds in a 180°C oven on a baking tray until golden. Cool and then blitz in a food processor to a fine powder. Lightly whip the cream and fold in the cool gooseberry liquor and almonds.

To assemble the tart, preheat the oven to 180°C and lightly grease a 10-inch flan dish with butter.

Roll the pastry into a ball. Lightly flour your work surface, then roll out the pastry, moving it around to prevent it from sticking, into a 12-inch circle. Line the flan dish with the pastry, allowing excess pastry to hang over the edges. Line the dish with cling film and fill with baking beans. Place on a baking tray and bake for 15 minutes. Remove the beans and cling film.

Allow the crust to cool, then spread a third of the frangipane on the bottom of the pastry sheet. Dot over the gooseberries and then spread over the remaining frangipane. Bake for 35 to 40 minutes, or until firm and golden to touch. Cool slightly, then cut into slices, with the almond cream served on the side.

a kitchen year

august

august

Gone are the days when barbecuing meant a few fatty sausages and the obligatory burgers thrown on a grill – and nine times out of ten, burnt on the outside and raw in the middle. Barbecuing food adds a delicious rich smokiness and we've really embraced this way of cooking. On dry days, the barbecue is an extension of the kitchen. Most food can be adapted for the barbecue – fish, meats, fruit, vegetables, even pizza.

While baking a cake is an exact science, barbecuing relies completely on getting a real 'feel' for the grill and the food you're cooking. Regardless of whether you're using a gas, instant or drum-style charcoal barbecue, get to know the hot and cool spots on your grill. Once you've mastered the heat spots, use them to your advantage – get a good 'sear' on meats or fish and then transfer them to the cooler area to cook through.

Over the years, I've tried barbecuing everything but the curtains! What I've learned is the importance of marinating meats, either in a dry rub or a wet marinade, and I've included examples of both in this chapter. Also, glazing as you grill – whether with your meats, fish or vegetables – will improve the flavour and appearance brilliantly. So even if you're just doing a few sausages, marinate them first and then brush with some sticky barbecue sauce to pep them up.

Every cook in the southern states of America has their own barbecue sauce recipe that they think is the best. I might not be American, but I've included my own personal, agonised-over and much-tweaked barbecue sauce (p. 120).

And not forgetting dessert, there are strawberries roasted with lemon and rosé wine and grilled pineapple, all done on the barbecue. And you can't go through August without an icy dessert, so there's frozen coconut mousse with blackcurrants.
So what are you waiting for? Get grilling!

grilled sea bass with artichoke and grilled lime relish and orange oil

Serves 4

Oily sea bass is ideal for barbecuing. I like to start it on the hot side of the barbecue to crisp up the skin, then transfer to a cooler side to slowly cook through (you could wrap it in tin foil to protect it completely – just turn it every now and then). Sharp, intense artichokes and citrus provide the perfect foil for this creamy, crisp fish.

Sea bass:
1 whole sea bass (about 750 g in weight),
  gutted
olive oil
salt and pepper

Artichoke and grilled lime relish:
1 tablespoon olive oil
2 shallots, peeled and finely chopped
1 clove garlic, crushed
50 ml vermouth
2 plum tomatoes
1 lime
½ teaspoon caster sugar
100 g grilled artichokes from a jar
handful fresh chopped flat leaf parsley
salt and pepper

Orange oil:
See p. 118.

To prepare the fish, first ask your fishmonger to scale the sea bass or do this yourself by scraping the scales off with the blunt edge of a knife (start at the tail and scrape towards the head). With sharp scissors, cut off the fins – be very careful, as the top dorsal is especially sharp. Score the skin in 3 places on each side. Brush with oil, season with salt and pepper and place on the hottest part of the barbecue. Cook for 1 minute on each side, then move to the coolest part of the barbecue and cook, turning over every couple of minutes, until the fish is firm to the touch, about 15 minutes.

To make the relish, heat the oil over a medium heat and add the shallots and garlic. Cook until soft. Add the vermouth and cook until all but a tablespoon of liquid remains.

Bring a pot of water to a rolling boil and have a bowl of iced water on the side. Score the top of the tomatoes and plunge into the boiling water. Leave for 10 seconds, then add to the cold water. Peel the tomatoes and cut into quarters. Scoop out the seeds. You can bag and freeze the seeds to use for soups or sauces in the future. Dice each quarter and add to the shallot mixture.

Cut the lime in half and brush the cut surfaces with oil. Grill the limes on the barbecue until they're marked. Squeeze the juice of the lime into the shallot mix and add the sugar. Roughly chop the artichokes and add to the relish with a little of the oil from the jar. Add the parsley and check the seasoning.

To serve, drizzle the orange oil on p. 118 over the grilled bass and serve the artichoke relish on the side.

orange oil

Makes 100 ml

Drying orange skin in the oven and grinding it to a fine powder is a great way of achieving an intense orange flavour. I use this for cakes and also in Asian-flavoured sauces to accompany pork or beef.

1 orange
100 ml olive oil

Preheat the oven to 100°C.

Peel the skin off the orange with a vegetable peeler. Scrape off any white pith from the inside of the skin, as this is bitter.

Place the pieces of skin on a tray lined with parchment paper and bake in the oven for about 1 hour, or until brittle and dry. Grind in a coffee grinder to a fine powder and mix with the oil. This will keep in the fridge for 2 months.

barbecued pizza with grilled chicken and Fontina cheese

Serves 4

Don't panic about the thought of pizza on the barbecue – just think of it as toasting bread (just a bit longer). The key is to use a medium-hot part of the barbecue so as not to burn the outside of the dough and leave the middle raw. Local tomatoes slowly 'melted' into a sauce with anchovies and olive oil make a sensuously sweet pizza sauce. Fontina cheese is a delicious, nutty Italian cheese that melts like a dream and is a change from the ubiquitous mozzarella.

Tomato sauce:
1 tablespoon olive oil
2 shallots, finely chopped
2 cloves garlic, crushed
250 g tomatoes, roughly chopped
1 anchovy, finely chopped (preferably a jarred, salted variety)
1 teaspoon sugar
1 tablespoon red wine vinegar
salt and pepper
2 tablespoons extra virgin olive oil
handful fresh chopped basil leaves

Marinated chicken:
1 tablespoon red wine vinegar
2 tablespoons olive oil
1 tablespoon chopped fresh oregano
2 chicken breasts
salt and pepper

1 batch pizza dough (see p. 73)
100 g Fontina cheese, sliced

To make the sauce, heat the olive oil in a saucepan over a medium heat. Add the shallots and garlic and cook until soft. Add the tomatoes, anchovy, sugar and red wine vinegar. Simmer on a low heat for 20 minutes. Check the seasoning and add the extra virgin olive oil and basil.

To prepare the chicken, mix the vinegar, oil and oregano together, pour over the chicken and cover. Refrigerate for at least 2 hours.

Season the chicken and grill on the barbecue until fully cooked. Set aside and rest, then cut into slices.

To complete the pizza, roll out the pizza dough to $\frac{1}{2}$ cm thick and place on a medium-hot barbecue. On a gas barbecue, turn the gas down or wait until the coals on a regular barbecue are starting to cool – check by placing a small amount of dough on the grill to test the heat. Cook until the dough starts to cook, then flip over. Cook until the dough is almost cooked through. Spread over the sauce, then dot the chicken all over the sauce. Spread the sliced cheese over the top of the pizza. Place a lid on the barbecue and cook for about 3 minutes, or until the cheese has melted. Remove from the grill and serve.

barbecued duck breast

Serves 4

Duck might not seem like the obvious thing to do on the barbecue, as it's quite fatty, but remove the fat, rub on a dry marinade and baste on the barbecue with this sticky sauce and it becomes a natural.

4 duck breasts
olive oil, for grilling
salt

Dry rub marinade:
1 teaspoon coriander seeds
1 teaspoon cumin seeds
1 teaspoon smoked paprika
½ teaspoon freshly ground black pepper

Barbecue sauce
1 tablespoon olive oil
½ small red onion, finely chopped
2 cloves garlic, chopped
1 green chilli, deseeded and chopped
100 ml Worcestershire sauce
100 ml passata
1 tablespoon tomato purée
100 ml cider
100 ml apple juice
100 ml chicken stock (see p. 11)
200 g soft brown sugar
2 tablespoons apple balsamic vinegar

To make the dry rub and prepare the duck, grind the seeds and mix with the smoked paprika and pepper. Remove the skin from the duck breasts and rub the spice blend all over the duck. Cover and refrigerate for at least 4 hours and up to 24 hours.

To make the barbecue sauce, heat the oil in a large saucepan over medium heat and add the onion, garlic and chilli. Cook for 10 minutes, stirring occasionally, then add the Worcestershire sauce, passata and tomato purée and cook for 5 minutes. Add the remaining ingredients and simmer for 30 minutes. Blend the sauce to a smooth purée, then pass through a sieve.

When ready to cook, brush the duck breasts lightly with olive oil and season with salt. Place on the barbecue and brush over 1 tablespoon of the sauce. After 2 minutes, turn over the duck and brush the other side with the sauce. Keep turning and brushing the duck until it's cooked to your liking – about 5 minutes for medium rare and up to 15 for well done. The firmer the duck breast feels, the more it is 'done'.

Allow to rest for 3 minutes before serving.

lamb kebabs with lemon and fenugreek and creamy tahini dressing

Serves 4

Sweet, succulent lamb infused with zingy lemons and the warmth of spicy fenugreek is only made better by grilling on a smoky barbecue. Tahini is a sesame seed paste and it makes a great base for a creamy yoghurt-based dressing.

For a fantastic accompaniment to this dish, make some of the naan breads on p. 136, but grill them on the barbecue instead of under the grill. Grilled pitta would also be great with the kebabs.

Lamb kebabs:
1 kg lean lamb cubes, prepared from leg meat
  (ask your butcher)
1 tablespoon fenugreek seeds
zest and juice of 2 lemons
1 tablespoon honey
2 cloves garlic
75 ml olive oil
2 onions
8 wooden skewers, soaked in cold water for 30
  minutes
salt and pepper

Creamy tahini dressing:
100 ml sour cream
2 tablespoons olive oil
juice of 1 lime or lemon
1 tablespoon tahini paste
handful fresh chopped coriander
2 cloves roasted garlic (see p. 8)
1 teaspoon honey
salt and pepper

To make the kebabs, place the lamb in a bowl. Grind the fenugreek seeds in a spice grinder or mortar and pestle to a fine powder. In a blender, process the fenugreek seeds, lemon zest and juice, honey, garlic and olive oil to a smooth purée. Mix this into the lamb, making sure it's all coated. Cover with cling film and refrigerate to marinate for at least 6 hours and preferably longer – up to 2 days.

Half an hour prior to cooking, remove the meat from the fridge. Peel the onions and cut in half through the root. Cut each half in half and then in half again. Break up the onions. Thread the lamb onto the skewers, alternating each piece with onion. Season well with salt and pepper. Barbecue for 10 to 15 minutes, turning frequently.

To make the dressing, whisk together all the ingredients and serve with the kebabs.

grilled polenta

Serves 4

While a steaming bowl of polenta will warm the cockles of your heart in mid-winter, chargrilling it is a sunny, smoky way of serving it.

Serve with the salsa rossa on p. 123, which is a brilliant way of bringing the best out of the crispy polenta.

2 tablespoons olive oil
1 small white onion, finely chopped
2 cloves garlic, crushed
1 litre chicken or vegetable stock (see p. 11)
300 g polenta
75 g grated fresh Parmesan cheese
oil, for grilling

To make the polenta, heat the oil in a large saucepan and add the onion and garlic. Cook over a medium heat until golden, then add the stock. Bring the stock to the boil, then slowly, whisking all the time, add the polenta. Be careful, as it can spit at you a bit! When fully incorporated, lower the heat and simmer for about 30 minutes, stirring frequently. If using instant polenta, which is more readily available, cook for 5 minutes. Add the Parmesan and the check seasoning.

Pour the polenta into a lightly greased tray and leave to set, about 30 minutes. When set, cut into the desired shapes and then brush lightly with oil. Cook on the hottest part of the grill for about 1 minute on each side.

Serve immediately with the salsa rossa on p. 123.

salsa rossa

Makes enough for 4 servings

Salsa rossa literally means 'red sauce'. This is good with grilled steaks, chicken or most grilled fish.

2 tablespoons olive oil
4 red peppers
1 red chilli
4 plum tomatoes
2 shallots, peeled and finely chopped
2 cloves garlic, crushed
salt and pepper
1 tablespoon red wine vinegar
juice of 1 lemon
2 tablespoons extra virgin olive oil
handful fresh chopped basil leaves
handful fresh chopped flat leaf parsley leaves

Preheat the oven to 200°C.

Use 1 tablespoon of olive oil to brush the red peppers and red chilli. Place in the oven and cook until scorched and blistered – the red peppers will take about 20 minutes, but remove the red chilli after just 1 minute. Place in a bowl, cover with cling film and set aside.

Bring a pot of water to a rolling boil. Score the tops of the tomatoes. Have a bowl of iced water standing by. Plunge the tomatoes into the boiling water for 10 seconds, then remove from the hot water with a slotted spoon and place in the iced water. Peel the tomatoes and discard the skin (or add it to stocks). Quarter the tomatoes and remove the seeds, placing the seeds in a separate bowl. Cut the tomato quarters into dice and set aside.

Heat the remaining tablespoon of olive oil in a saucepan over a medium heat and add the shallots and garlic. Cook until golden, then add the tomato seeds and season well with salt and pepper. Simmer for 20 minutes, then pass through a sieve into a bowl. Peel and deseed the red peppers and chilli and chop into ½ cm pieces. Add to the tomato 'sauce' with the chopped tomatoes, red wine vinegar, lemon juice, extra virgin olive oil, basil and parsley. Check the seasoning and serve at room temperature.

barbecued halloumi cheese, courgettes and piquillo rolls with a garlic, chilli and fennel dressing

Serves 4

Halloumi is a hard Cypriot cheese that is ideal for grilling, as it holds its shape when heated.

2 large courgettes
2 tablespoons olive oil
salt and pepper
200 g halloumi cheese, sliced into 12 sticks
1 teaspoon smoked paprika
1 tablespoon olive oil
12 piquillo peppers
handful fresh basil

To make the courgettes, slice each of the courgettes lengthwise into 6 slices. Brush with the oil and season with salt and pepper. Grill on the barbecue until marked and golden.

Toss the halloumi in the smoked paprika and oil. Cook on the barbecue until marked.

Place a grilled courgette slice on a work surface and place a piece of halloumi at one end. Place a piquillo on top of the cheese and then a leaf of basil. Roll up around the halloumi. Repeat with the other slices of courgette. Place on a platter.

Garlic, chilli and fennel dressing:
1 tablespoon olive oil
2 cloves garlic, chopped
1 shallot, finely chopped
1 red chilli, deseeded and chopped
½ bulb fennel, core removed and finely chopped
juice of 1 lemon
½ teaspoon salt
100 ml dry white wine
1 tablespoon white wine vinegar
50 ml olive oil

Heat the tablespoon of oil in a saucepan over a medium heat. Add the garlic, shallot and chilli and cook for 2 minutes. Toss the chopped fennel in the lemon juice and add to the shallot mixture. Season with salt. Add the white wine and simmer until the fennel is soft, about 5 minutes. Cool, then add the vinegar and 50 ml of olive oil. Blend to a smooth dressing and check the seasoning. Drizzle over the courgette rolls and serve.

roast strawberries

Serves 4

1 lemongrass stalk
1 vanilla pod
200 g caster sugar
juice and zest of 1 lemon
100 ml rosé or white wine
500 g strawberries
splash of limoncello, to finish

Top and tail the lemongrass. Remove the outer tough leaves and chop the lemongrass as finely as you can. Place the lemongrass in a saucepan. Split the vanilla pod and scrape the seeds into the saucepan with the lemongrass and add the sugar, lemon juice, zest and wine. Simmer until the sugar has dissolved, then allow to infuse for at least 4 hours.

To finish on the barbecue, take a large sheet of tin foil and place the strawberries in the middle. Gather up the sides of the foil and pour over the syrup. Tightly enclose the strawberries and place on the barbecue for 10 minutes. Open up the foil, empty the strawberries into a bowl to serve and drizzle over the limoncello.

Serve the strawberries with ice cream or sorbet. Any leftover juices can be added to chilled sparkling wine to make a fantastically aromatic cocktail.

grilled pineapple with lime sugar

Serves 4

The natural sugars in pineapple make it ideal for grilling, giving it a great candied flavour. Grilled pineapple is grand on its own as a finishing touch to a barbecue, but dipping it into zingy lime sugar is a bit of fun, like sherbet dib-dabs for the Noughties!

The lime sugar will keep in an airtight container for up to 1 month and is also good sprinkled over fresh berries or peaches.

2 limes
100 g caster sugar
1 large pineapple

To make the lime sugar, preheat the oven to 100°C. Peel each lime with a potato peeler and scrape off any of the white pith. Place the peel on a baking tray lined with non-stick parchment paper. Cook for about 45 minutes, or until the lime peel is dried out completely. Cool and grind in a coffee grinder. Combine with the sugar and set aside until ready to use.

Peel the pineapple and carefully remove the 'eyes'. Cut the pineapple in half from top to bottom and then cut each half in half.

Remove the core from each quarter. Cut each quarter in half through the middle and then cut each piece into 3 wedges.

Place on a white hot barbecue and cook for 1 minute on each side, or until marked golden brown.

Serve the lime sugar in a bowl with the pineapple wedges on the side.

frozen toasted coconut mousse with blackcurrant compote

Serves 4

My mother made a dessert a few years ago that combined fresh blackcurrants and coconut. I was a bit sceptical about this flavour combination, but surprisingly, it works really well. This dessert is essentially an ice cream made with a coconut cream custard infused with that old 1980s favourite, Malibu. Secretly, I still love Malibu, so this dessert is the perfect excuse to have it in the drinks cupboard. Blackcurrants are one of the great unsung heroes of the fruit world. We're far more interested in importing goji berries from far-flung places than recognising the superfood right on our doorstep. And besides, they taste stunning! For a simple dessert, combine the blackcurrant compote with lightly whipped cream to make an ethereal summer pudding, but for something more special, this really is the business.

Coconut mousse:
4 large egg yolks
100 g caster sugar
75 ml whole milk
75 ml coconut cream (available in small cartons and not to be confused with creamed coconut – use coconut milk as a substitute)
75 ml Malibu or regular rum
2 tablespoons honey
50 g desiccated coconut
250 ml double cream
zest of 1 lime

Blackcurrant compote:
250 g blackcurrants
75 g sugar
juice of 1 lemon

To make the mousse, preheat the oven to 200°C.

Whisk the egg yolks, sugar, milk, coconut cream, rum and honey in a glass or metal bowl. Place this over a pot of simmering water and continue to whisk constantly, until the mixture becomes thick, creamy and feels hot when you stick your finger into it, about 10 minutes. Remove from the heat and stir occasionally until the mixture is cool.

Sprinkle the desiccated coconut on a baking tray. Cook until golden – check this frequently, as it will burn easily – approximately 5 minutes. Cool.

Lightly whisk the cream to soft peaks and fold this into the cold coconut custard. Fold in the toasted coconut and lime zest.

Lightly oil a loaf tin and line with cling film. Pour the mousse into this and cover with more cling film. Freeze for 6 hours. When ready to serve, remove from the freezer 5 minutes before serving, then pull out of the tin. Remove cling film and cut into wedges. Alternatively, pour the mousse into individual moulds and freeze.

To make the compote, pick over the blackcurrants to remove any stems or stray leaves. Wash in cold water and place in a saucepan with the sugar and lemon juice. Simmer gently until the blackcurrants are slightly soft. Cool.

To serve, place each slice of mousse or individual mousse on a plate, spoon the compote around and dust with icing sugar.

september

september

Despite the fact that September signifies a few depressing things for many people – cooler, shorter evenings, kids back to school, hot summer holidays gone – it's an exciting time food wise. At this time of year, I've had enough of cold salads and cold food. Now is the time to indulge in some warm, spicy, borderline comfort food.

When cooking with spices, your best bet is to buy small packs of whole seeds and then grind them yourself. Either use a mortar and pestle to grind spices or buy a coffee bean grinder and use it exclusively for spices (ground coffee vaguely tainted with cumin is not a good wake-up call!). Personally, I think life is too short to use a mortar and pestle when an electric coffee grinder will do the job in a tenth of the time, but the choice is yours. I buy small amounts of spices to ensure freshness. The longer spices hang around, the less pungency they have and in turn your finished dish will lack the punch it should have.

To finish off a spicy meal, what could be better than a soothingly lush mango? September brings with it the short season of Alphonse mangoes – these have an intense sweetness and a chin-soaking juiciness. Make the most of them and then, when you've eaten your fill, blend the pulp and freeze in bags to brighten up a dull winter day. Greengages – sweet green plums – are also around now for a limited time. You could use them in a tart or pie, but I like to preserve them by making them into a spicy chutney to serve with cold meats or duck. Another great preserve is mint and green chilli jelly – why waste all that abundance of late summer mint? And if you're not naturally inclined towards jam making, get yourself in the mood with a passionfruit daiquiri!

butternut squash and garam masala fritters with cumin yoghurt dressing

Serves 4

These sunny little bites take their inspiration from onion bhajis (salting the squash to draw out the moisture and then using the liquid to make a batter with gram flour). The sweetness of the fritter is balanced beautifully with the spices, chilli and tang of the yoghurt.

Cumin yoghurt dressing:
1 dessertspoon cumin seeds
200 ml full-fat yoghurt
2 finely chopped scallions
2 cloves roasted garlic (see p. 8)
handful fresh coriander, finely chopped
salt and pepper

Fritters:
250 g peeled and coarsely grated butternut
  squash
1 medium white onion, peeled and finely sliced
1 teaspoon salt
1 teaspoon garam masala
1 clove garlic, crushed
1 teaspoon chopped green chilli
2 tablespoons chopped fresh coriander
1 teaspoon finely grated ginger
125 g gram flour
1 medium egg
½ teaspoon baking powder
vegetable oil for frying

To make the dressing, toast the cumin seeds in a dry frying pan until they start to pop. Mix with the other ingredients and set aside.

To make the fritters, place the butternut squash, onions and salt in a bowl and stir around to disperse the salt. Set aside and leave for 20 minutes.

Cook the garam masala in a dry pan for few seconds to release the aroma. Add this to the butternut mixture with the garlic, chilli, coriander and ginger. Mix well and then add the gram flour, egg and baking powder. Fold all the ingredients together.

Heat about a thumbnail's depth of vegetable oil in a frying pan over a medium heat. Add dessertspoon-size drops of the batter to the pan and cook for about 2 minutes, then flip over and repeat on the other side. Drain on kitchen paper. Serve immediately with the dressing.

spiced creamy lentil salad

Serves 4

Lentils have had a bit of a renaissance lately, managing to shake off their 1970s hippy image. I love Puy lentils, as they retain a bit of bite and are a great vehicle for spices. This is great as a vegetarian side dish but would also work well with grilled chicken, meats or oily fish.

1 tablespoon vegetable oil
1 small white onion, peeled and finely chopped
1 clove crushed garlic
1 teaspoon grated fresh ginger
50 g celery, finely diced
1 teaspoon ground coriander
½ teaspoon ground cumin
4 green cardamom pods, seeds removed
1 teaspoon garam masala
200 g Puy lentils, washed
300 ml vegetable stock
100 ml passata
200 g cherry tomatoes, halved
handful fresh chopped coriander
100 ml sour cream
salt and pepper

Heat the oil in a large saucepan over a medium heat. Add the onion, garlic, ginger and celery. Cook until soft, about 5 minutes. Add the coriander, cumin, the seeds from the cardamom pods and garam masala and cook for 1 minute. Add the lentils, stock and passata and simmer for 20 minutes, or until the lentils have absorbed all the liquid but still have a bit of a bite when tasted. Remove from the heat and add the tomatoes and coriander. Cool slightly, add the sour cream and check the seasoning. Serve straight away or chill until needed.

tandoori-baked chicken

Serves 4

This is my version of a classic and is far removed from the artificial coloured pastes available commercially. Adding red pepper to the paste isn't very traditional, but it gives the dish a sweetness that cuts through the sultriness of the spices and chilli. The spice blend also works well for baking salmon or lamb. Grinding spice seeds gives a more pungent taste, but substitute ready-ground for handiness.

Serve this with the naan bread on p. 136.

1 teaspoon coriander seeds

1 teaspoon fennel seeds

1 teaspoon fenugreek seeds

6 cardamom pods

½ teaspoon cumin seeds

½ teaspoon ground cinnamon

½ teaspoon ground turmeric

1 red chilli, chopped (remove the seeds for a less hot version)

1 red pepper, seeds removed and roughly chopped

1 onion, peeled and chopped

2 cloves garlic, peeled and chopped

50 g grated fresh ginger

2 tomatoes, roughly chopped

200 ml natural yoghurt

1 teaspoon salt

1 teaspoon caster sugar

4 chicken breasts

chopped fresh coriander, to garnish

steamed or boiled rice, to serve

naan bread, to serve (see p. 136)

Toast the coriander seeds, fennel seeds, fenugreek seeds, cardamom pods and cumin seeds in a dry frying pan until they start to pop. Lightly press the cardamom pods to remove the outer husk and place them with the other spices. Grind in either a mortar and pestle or a coffee grinder to a fine powder.

In a blender, process the spices with all the other ingredients (except the chicken) to a smooth paste. Pour over the chicken breasts and leave to marinate in the fridge for at least 24 hours and up to 72 hours.

Preheat the oven to 200°C.

Lightly oil a baking dish and place the chicken in the dish. Cover with the marinade and bake for 20 minutes. Garnish with fresh coriander and serve with steamed or boiled rice and naan bread.

naan bread

Makes 8 naans

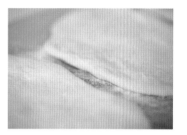

Naan bread involves a little bit of effort, but the results are spectacular.

225 g self-raising flour
1 teaspoon salt
2 tablespoons full-fat yoghurt
100 ml lukewarm water

Place the flour, salt and yoghurt in a bowl and add the water a little at a time, mixing all the time until you have a sticky dough. Knead the dough for a minute and then place in a bowl and cover with a damp tea towel. Leave in a warm place for about 1 hour.

Divide the dough into 8 pieces. Form each piece into a ball and then roll out into an oval shape. Repeat with all 8 pieces.

Place the naans under a hot grill until they puff up and are mottled and brown, about 30 seconds, then flip over and cook on the other side.

Serve warm either as they are, or mix 1 tablespoon of chopped coriander into 2 tablespoons of olive oil and brush this over the naans as they're ready. You could also rub over some roasted garlic or toast a tablespoon of black onion seeds in a dry frying pan until they pop and add to a tablespoon of olive oil to brush over.

halibut baked in muhammara

Serves 4

Muhammara is a Middle Eastern dip or sauce. It's a combination of roasted peppers, walnuts, cumin and pomegranate molasses.

Pomegranate molasses is an exotic, thick, sweet and sour syrup. Muhammara is great served with vegetables or pitta to dip. But where it really becomes something special is smeared on fish and then baked in a hot oven. Halibut really suits the muhammara, but I've also done it successfully with salmon and mackerel.

**4 x 200 g pieces of halibut, preferably around
 2 cm thick**

Muhammara:
oil, for brushing
2 red peppers
1 red chilli (optional)
50 g walnuts, roughly chopped
1 heaped teaspoon cumin seeds
juice of 1 lemon
1 tablespoon pomegranate molasses
1 tablespoon walnut oil
2 tablespoons olive oil
handful fresh chopped coriander
salt and pepper
baby potatoes or rice, to serve

Preheat the oven to 200°C.

Brush the red peppers with oil and bake in the oven for 10 minutes. Brush the chilli with oil and add to the peppers. When the skin of the peppers and chilli is scorched, cool them slightly, then peel and deseed them.

Toast the walnuts and cumin seeds in a dry frying pan for 30 seconds.

Blend the red peppers, chillies, walnuts, cumin seeds, lemon juice, pomegranate molasses, walnut oil, olive oil and coriander. Season with salt and pepper.

Lightly brush a baking tray with oil. Place the halibut on the tray and smear the muhamarra on top of the fish.

Bake at 200°C for approximately 15 minutes. To check if it's ready, squeeze the sides – they should be firm but with a little give.

Serve with some baby potatoes or rice.

mint and green chilli jelly

Makes 4 x 250 g jars

I have a pot in the garden that absolutely bursts with mint in the summer. Mint has a tendency to take over a garden, so this recipe is a great way to use it up. Making jelly is such a satisfying thing – taking mint, combining it with some simple ingredients and ending up with jewel-like clear green jars of something very special. The first time I made this jelly, I was so proud I couldn't stop looking at it! Mint jelly makes a great gift and is gorgeous with spiced or roast lamb.

525 g granulated sugar
2 big bunches of mint
200 ml water
100 ml white wine vinegar
1 deseeded green chilli
75 ml pectin
3 drops green food colouring

Place the sugar in a non-reactive saucepan. Pick the mint leaves off the stalks and add to the sugar. Crush the mint into the sugar with the end of a rolling pin or back of a spoon to release the flavours. Add the water and vinegar. Bring to the boil and simmer for 2 minutes. Add the chilli and boil for 2 minutes. Add the pectin and food colouring and boil rapidly for 1 minute. While hot, strain the liquid through muslin or a blue J-cloth into a clean jug.

Sterilise 4 jam jars by placing them on a tray in a 200°C oven for 10 minutes. Add the strained jelly into the jars and place the lid on tightly. Place the jars in a pot of boiling water and simmer for 10 minutes, making sure the jars are submerged in the water. Remove from the pot and cool. Stored unopened in a cool dark place, the jelly will keep for a year.

spiced greengage chutney

Makes 4 x 250 g jars

Greengages are largely ignored in favour of their more colourful purple cousins, the plums. This is a shame, as they have a lovely old-fashioned plum taste combined with a vibrant green flesh. Like plums, they're great in both desserts and spicy chutneys.

1 tablespoon olive oil
3 shallots, peeled and finely chopped
50 g ginger, peeled and finely grated
½ cinnamon stick
½ teaspoon ground cloves
seeds from 6 cardamom pods
150 g golden caster sugar
100 ml cider vinegar
1 kg greengages, cut in half, stone removed
    and then cut in quarters

Heat the oil in a large saucepan over a medium heat and add the shallots and ginger. Cook until soft, about 5 minutes. Add the cinnamon stick, ground cloves and cardamom seeds. Cook for 30 seconds, then add the sugar and vinegar. Simmer for 2 minutes, then add the greengages. Simmer for a further 20 minutes on a low heat, stirring occasionally.

Sterilise 4 x 250 g jam jars by placing them on a tray in a 200°C oven for 10 minutes. Pour the chutney into the jars and place the lids on tightly. Place the jars in a pot of boiling water and simmer for 10 minutes, making sure the jars are submerged in the water. Remove from the pot and cool.

Stored unopened in a cool dark place, the chutney will keep for up to a year, or refrigerate for up to 2 weeks once opened.

mango and lime biscuit bars

Serves 4

Mango and lime are perfect for each other. These biscuits combine slowly cooked ripe mangoes with tangy lime, sandwiched between coconut shortbread. Don't panic about rolling out shortbread – in this recipe, you simply grate the set shortbread dough. If you want to make it even easier, replace the mango mixture with raspberry or apricot jam.

200 g butter, softened
150 g caster sugar
2 large egg yolks
150 g plain flour
1 teaspoon baking powder
50 g desiccated coconut
2 ripe mangoes
zest and juice of 2 limes
75 g caster sugar
1 tablespoon water

Preheat the oven to 180°C.

Beat the butter and 150 g caster sugar together until pale and fluffy. Add the egg yolks and mix well. Sift in the flour, baking powder and coconut. Mix to a soft dough. Divide the dough in two and wrap up each piece in cling film. Chill for 1 hour, or until hard.

Peel the mangoes and cut the flesh away from the husk in the middle. Chop into 1 cm dice and place in a saucepan with the lime zest and juice, sugar and water. Simmer for 30 minutes, or until the mango is soft and the liquid is syrupy. Cool completely.

Butter a square or rectangular baking dish. Grate one half of the hard dough onto the bottom, ensuring all the corners are filled. Spread the mango mix on top, then grate the remaining half of the dough onto the mango. Spread over evenly. Bake for 30 minutes, or until golden and firm. Cool, then slice into bar shapes.

passionfruit daiquiris

Serves 4

Daiquiris remind me of college in America, big hair and shoulder pads! Big hair might be making a bit of a comeback, so there's hope for this drink as well (it tastes so good, it deserves a second chance).

100 g golden caster sugar
150 ml water
4 passionfruit
juice of 2 limes
100 ml white rum
handful ice cubes
fresh mint, to garnish

Boil the sugar and water in a heavy-based saucepan until the sugar has dissolved. Cool.

Cut the passionfruit in half and scoop the seeds into a sieve placed over a bowl. Press the pulp to release as much of the juice as possible. Add the lime juice to the passionfruit juice. Place in a jug blender with the sugar solution, rum and ice and blend to a slush. Pour into iced martini glasses and garnish with some fresh mint.

october

october

The last bastions of summer are coming to an exquisite end now. Local tomatoes, raspberries, blackberries and elderberries are at the end of their season and are at their intense best as autumn creeps in. An ideal way of preserving tomatoes is to make the melted tomato sauce on p. 119 and freeze it in bags or bottle it to enjoy throughout the winter with pasta or in soups. And of course you can freeze or make jam from all those berries.

Elderberries make a great jelly and their intense, tongue-puckering sourness can be pepped up with lots of sugar and sweet port.

October is a great month to batten down the hatches and enjoy some comfort food. As a lifetime lover of a good soup, now is the time to make up for the lack of fresh delicate vegetables and leaves with a big rustic soup with warm, fresh bread straight from the oven to mop up the last drops in the bowl.

When I was growing up, we lived beside a quarry full of hazelnut trees and the sweet, fresh nuts that we picked were a real treat. Plums and damsons are also in season and roasting them in a spice-infused winey syrup is a perfect way to serve them. A cake baked full of freshly shelled hazelnuts is a perfect, creamy foil to the astringent red fruits.

rustic bean soup with tomatoes and smoked bacon

Serves 4

My grandparents used to grow the best tomatoes, and to this day, whenever I walk into a greenhouse full of the intoxicating smell of the sweet fruit, I'm transported back 30 years. My favourite time to eat local tomatoes is at the end of the season, in October. These home-grown tomatoes are as far removed from the supermarket variety as I am from Kate Moss! Every patch of their knobbly, mottled skin tells a story. While just great on their own with some toasted foccacia and a liberal dose of good olive oil and garlic, adding them to a rustic soup is probably more fitting to the weather. Use any beans you like here, though I personally like borlotti.

250 g dried borlotti beans, soaked in cold
   water overnight
sprigs fresh thyme and rosemary
4 cloves garlic, peeled
1 tablespoon olive oil
4 rashers smoked streaky bacon
1 medium white onion
75 g chopped celery
250 g tomatoes, roughly chopped
1 litre chicken stock (see p. 11)
handful fresh chopped flat leaf parsley
good olive oil, for garnishing

Drain the soaked borlotti beans and place in a saucepan. Cover with cold water, add the thyme and rosemary and 1 of the cloves of garlic (cut in half). Bring to the boil and simmer until the beans are soft, about 30 minutes. Drain.

Heat the oil in a large saucepan. Chop the bacon into 1 cm thick strips and add to the oil when hot. Cook until golden, then remove from the pan and set aside. Chop the remaining garlic and add to the saucepan with the onion and celery. Cook on a low heat until the vegetables have softened, about 10 minutes. Add half the tomatoes, the stock and half the cooked beans. Simmer for 10 minutes. Blend the soup in a liquidiser – don't bother straining, as it's a rustic soup anyway.

Return to the pan and add the remaining tomatoes. Simmer for 5 minutes, then add the remaining beans and cooked bacon and simmer for a further 5 minutes. Add the parsley, pour into bowls and drizzle over a bit of oil. Serve with crisp warm bread.

You could also scatter over a bit of freshly grated Parmesan or keep the whole thing local and grate over some hard Gabriel cheese instead.

mussels baked with herby hazelnut, garlic and cider crumbs

Serves 4

This may be a fiddly dish to make, but it's an awful lot easier to eat. The taste of grilled mussels topped with buttery crumbs is hard to resist. These also make great finger food for a party.

1 kg mussels, scrubbed clean
1 tablespoon olive oil
1 shallot, finely chopped
2 cloves garlic, crushed
200 ml dry cider
handful fresh chopped flat leaf parsley leaves
  (reserve the stalks for the cooking liquid)
50 g butter
60 g hazelnuts, chopped
100 g breadcrumbs
salt and pepper
good-quality olive oil, to garnish

Preheat the oven to 220°C.

Ensure the mussels are tightly shut. Tap an open one, and if it doesn't clam shut immediately, chuck it out.

Heat the oil in a large saucepan over a medium heat and add the shallot and garlic. Cook until golden, then add the cider and parsley stalks. Bring to the boil and add the mussels. Cover with a lid and cook for about 3 minutes, or until the mussels are open. Drain over a bowl to retain the cooking liquid.

Carefully remove the mussels from their shells and return to one half of the shell. Line up on a baking sheet.

Bring the cooking liquid to the boil and reduce to a thick sauce, about 5 minutes. Add the butter over a low heat until melted, then remove from the heat and add the hazelnuts, chopped parsley leaves and breadcrumbs. Check the seasoning, then pile the crumbs on top of each mussel. Bake the mussels for 5 minutes. Serve immediately, drizzled with good olive oil.

venison casserole with smoked shallots, beetroot and blackberry-infused ale

Serves 4

This casserole ticks all the comfort food boxes for me – dark, luscious meat, smoky shallots, intense sweet beetroot, berries and ale. Clotworthy Dobbin Ale is a brilliant ale from Kilkeel in Northern Ireland, but you can use any ale.

Oak chips can be bought in hardware/DIY shops or in the barbecue section of supermarkets.

1 cup oak chips
250 g shallots
250 g blackberries
1 tablespoon honey
300 ml Clotworthy Dobbin Ale (or any ale)
1 tablespoon olive oil
25 g butter
1 kg venison shoulder or stew cut, cut into
  2 cm chunks
salt and freshly ground black pepper
2 red onions, peeled and finely sliced
1 tablespoon chopped fresh thyme leaves
250 ml beef stock (make as for lamb stock on
  p. 57, or use 1 cube)
200 g cocktail beetroot
2 juniper berries
pared rind of orange, peeled with a vegetable
  peeler
mashed potatoes, to serve
red cabbage pickle, to serve (see p. 153)

Line a roasting tin with tin foil and sprinkle over the oak chips. Peel the shallots and cut in half through the root. Place a rack on top of the tray of oak chips and place the shallots on the rack. Cover the roasting tray tightly with tin foil and place directly onto a cooking ring. Cook for 5 minutes, then leave uncovered for 10 minutes.

Place the blackberries, honey and ale in a saucepan and simmer for 10 minutes. Set aside.

Heat the oil and butter in a casserole dish, and when foaming, add the venison and season with salt and pepper. Leave for 2 minutes, then turn over to seal the other side of the venison. Add the onions and cook for 5 minutes. Add the thyme. Press the blackberry ale mixture through a sieve onto the venison, squeezing out as much of the liquid as you can. Add the stock, beetroot, whole juniper berries and orange rind. Add to the casserole, place a lid on the whole thing and simmer very gently for 2 hours. Check every now and then and add a little water or stock if it starts to go dry. Check the seasoning and remove the juniper berries and orange rind.

Serve with mashed potatoes or the red cabbage on p. 153.

turnip and roast garlic gratin

Serves 4

When I was young (and this was a time when McDonald's was 3,000 miles away!), my favourite dinner was sausage, turnip and mash. While my pallet has become slightly more sophisticated, my love of turnip has never diminished. This is a variation on a dish my Aunt Doreen makes and is great served with roast beef or duck.

1 medium turnip, peeled and coarsely grated
salt and pepper
4 rashers smoked streaky bacon, cut into 1 cm strips
25 g butter
1 white onion, finely sliced
350 ml double cream
4 cloves roast garlic (see p. 8)
1 teaspoon fresh chopped thyme leaves
150 g grated Gruyère cheese
50 g breadcrumbs
Preheat the oven to 190°C.

Place the turnip in a large saucepan, cover with cold water, season with salt and pepper and bring to the boil. Simmer until cooked, about 5 minutes, and drain well. Place in a bowl.

Heat a large frying pan and when smoking, add the bacon and cook until golden. Add the butter and onion and cook on a low heat until the onion is soft, about 5 minutes. Add the cream and season with salt and pepper, though taste it first, as the bacon can be salty. Add the roast garlic and stir until fully mixed in. Add the thyme.

Mix with the turnip and turn into a lightly buttered oven dish. Mix the Gruyère and breadcrumbs and sprinkle over the top. Bake for 20 minutes, or until golden and bubbly.

red cabbage pickle

Serves 4

I lived in the North of England for a few years and grew to love Lancashire hotpot. While gorgeous on its own, pickled red cabbage gave it a lovely tangy lift. This red cabbage is also terrific served hot with casseroles or roasts, especially roast duck, or with cold meats.

1 medium red cabbage
1 Granny Smith apple
juice of 1 lemon
2 tablespoons olive oil
1 medium white onion, peeled and finely sliced
75 g Demerara sugar
salt and pepper
6 cardamom pods
½ cinnamon stick
pinch nutmeg
1 teaspoon ground coriander
1 star anise
500 ml dry red wine (I find a peppery Shiraz does the trick)
50 ml red wine vinegar
25 g raisins

Quarter the red cabbage, remove the cores and slice as thinly as you can. Peel, quarter and core the apples. Chop into thin slices and toss in the lemon juice.

Heat the oil in a large saucepan and add the onion, cooking on a low heat until it's golden brown, about 10 minutes. Add the sugar and cabbage and stir frequently until the cabbage has softened slightly, about 5 minutes. Season with salt and pepper.

Split the cardamom pods open, remove the seeds, crush them slightly with a rolling pin and add to the cabbage with the cinnamon stick, nutmeg, coriander and star anise. Add the wine, vinegar and raisins.

At the point, you can transfer the mixture to a casserole dish and bake at 160°C for 2 hours or cover and simmer until the cabbage is soft, about 40 minutes. Check the seasoning and serve immediately, or keep in the fridge for up to a week.

guinness, walnut and apple bread

Makes 1 loaf

Try to use fresh walnuts for this bread. They're in season now and vastly superior to pre-packed ones. The oil in walnuts tends to go rancid quite quickly, so if using packed walnuts, give them a good sniff – if they smell like a dirty chip pan, throw them out. The stout and apples complement the nuts beautifully. This bread, while sublime eaten freshly baked, is also great toasted as an accompaniment to a ripe blue cheese.

1 kg strong bread flour
2 sachets instant yeast
1 teaspoon salt
75 g finely chopped walnuts
100 ml Guinness
1 tablespoon honey
1 Granny Smith apple, grated
500 ml lukewarm water

Mix the flour, yeast, salt and walnuts in a large bowl.

In a separate bowl, mix the Guinness, honey and apple together.

Make a well in the middle of the dry ingredients and pour in the Guinness mixture. Add the water and mix to a loose dough.

Turn onto a floured surface and knead the dough for 10 minutes, or until it feels like elastic when stretched. Turn into a lightly oiled bowl, cover with a damp tea towel and leave in a warm place for 1 hour.

Preheat the oven to 190°C. Remove the dough from the bowl and turn onto a floured surface. Knead for 10 seconds, then either form into a large ball or a roughly shaped baguette, or divide into 2 and place in 2 lightly oiled and floured loaf tins. If making free-form bread, place on a lightly floured baking tray. Leave for 15 minutes, then bake for 40 to 50 minutes, or until the bread sounds hollow when the bottom is tapped.

Place on a wire rack and cool slightly before slicing.

elderberry and port jelly

Makes 4 x 250 g jars

What is it about elderberries? People have no qualms about using the flowers for cordials, infusions and even fritters, but the elderberries themselves are largely ignored. Apart from looking like clusters of fine gems, they have a tart, intense zing when tasted. Making a sweet jelly with elderberries and port is my favourite way of preparing them. Serve this with smoked duck at Christmas or eat now with ham or venison.

1 kg elderberries
1 litre port
500 g Granny Smith apples, unpeeled, chopped
  into small pieces
juice and zest of 1 lemon
450 g granulated sugar for every 500 ml
  extracted liquid
1 teaspoon butter

Remove the berries from their stalks with a fork and place in a large saucepan or jam pan. Add the port. Add the chopped apples to the pan with the lemon zest and juice and simmer for 1 hour, or until everything has broken down.

Suspend a jelly bag over a bowl, pour the elderberry mixture in and allow to trickle through overnight.

Place 3 saucers in the freezer.

Measure the liquid and weigh out 450 g of granulated sugar for every 500 ml of liquid. Place the sugar and liquid into a saucepan and bring to the boil. Add the butter and simmer for 30 minutes. Take a spoonful of the mixture and place on a cold saucer – if it solidifies, then it's ready.

Sterilise 4 jam jars by placing them on a tray in a 200°C oven for 10 minutes. Pour the jelly into the jars and place the lids on tightly.

Place a disc of greaseproof paper on top and cover with cling film or cellophane. Allow to set. Alternatively, place the jars in a pot of boiling water and simmer for 10 minutes, making sure the jars are submerged in the water. Remove from the pot and cool.

Stored in a cool dark place, this will keep for up to a year.

blackberry and Barolo sorbet

Serves 4

As a child, I spent most of the end of September and all of October with a purple moustache, caused by the stain of freshly picked blackberries. The purple moustache was often accompanied by a purple bum, caused by nettle stings trying to get at the prized berries, but it was a small price to pay for these free treats. Nowadays, I buy the blackberries already picked and combine them with Barolo wine to enjoy in a grown-up sorbet.

500 ml Barolo red wine (or your favourite red)
150 g sugar
1 tablespoon liquid glucose
zest and juice of 1 lemon
250 g blackberries

Boil the wine in a heavy-based saucepan until the liquid has reduced by half. Add the sugar, glucose, lemon zest and juice and bring to the boil. Simmer until the sugar has dissolved.

Add the blackberries and simmer until they become soft and burst. Blitz the mixture in a blender and then pass through a fine-mesh sieve. Cool.

If you're lucky enough to own an ice cream maker, churn it in the machine. If, like me, you don't own an ice cream maker, turn the mixture into a wide plastic container and freeze for 1 hour. Fluff up the mixture with a fork, then repeat this a couple of times every 15 minutes. This should prevent ice crystals forming and leave you with a smooth sorbet.

white chocolate and lemon crème brûlée with raspberries

Serves 4

Like tomatoes, local raspberries are at their finest now, taking on a deep, almost decadent quality. They have a rich, red hue and the taste is intense and sweet. As the American writer E.W. Howe put it, 'There is something in the red of a raspberry that looks as good to man as the red in a sheep looks to a wolf.' A creamy, wobbly crème brulée infused with lemon and chocolate is something sexy enough to do these tarty small fruits justice!

If buying a blowtorch to use in the kitchen, it's best to get one from a DIY shop, as they are more powerful than domestic ones and are cheaper too.

300 ml double cream
50 ml whole milk
1 vanilla pod
zest of 1 lemon
50 g good-quality white chocolate, chopped
3 large egg yolks
50 g caster sugar
100 g raspberries

Preheat the oven to 140°C.

Place the cream and milk in a saucepan. Split the vanilla pod lengthways and scrape the seeds into the pan. Add the pod and the lemon zest. Gently scald over a low heat. When hot, remove from the heat and add the chocolate, stirring until it's melted.

Whisk the egg yolks and sugar until pale. Strain the hot cream mixture through a fine sieve into the egg and sugar mix and whisk well.

Place the raspberries in the bottom of 4 large ramekins or coffee cups. Pour over the custard mix.

Place a folded tea towel in a roasting tray, place the ramekins on top and fill the tray halfway up the sides of the ramekins with boiling water.

Bake for approximately 40 minutes, or until the custard feels set when you touch the top but still has a wobble when you shake the ramekin gently. When ready, remove from the tray, cool and refrigerate for a couple of hours.

When ready to serve, evenly sprinkle caster sugar over the surface and either grill or use a blowtorch to caramelise the sugar.

hazelnut pound cake with spice-roasted plums

Serves 4

While a fragrant plum is a taste sensation, poaching them brings them to new heights. Pound cake is an American dish that's traditionally made with a pound each of butter, eggs and flour. The smell of a buttery cake baking is intoxicating anyway, but add toasted hazelnuts to the mix and you have something downright wicked.

Serve the cake while still warm with the plums and a good dollop of cream, or the cinnamon mascarpone on p. 31.

Hazelnut pound cake:
150 g skinned hazelnuts
250 g butter, at room temperature
250 g caster sugar
3 medium eggs
250 g sifted plain flour
1 teaspoon baking powder
1 teaspoon vanilla extract
zest of 1 orange (reserve the juice)

Spice-roasted plums:
8 plums, halved and stones removed
350 ml red wine
300 ml water
150 g caster sugar
1 cinnamon stick
pinch nutmeg
2 cloves
25 g grated fresh ginger root
reserved orange juice
1 star anise

To make the cake, preheat the oven to 180°C.

Place the hazelnuts on a roasting tray and cook until golden, about 10 minutes. Cool and then grind finely in a food processor. (Alternatively, you can buy ready-roasted hazelnuts in most supermarkets.)

Whisk the butter and sugar until pale and fluffy. Add the eggs one at a time, mixing well between each addition. When fully incorporated, fold in the flour, baking powder, ground nuts, vanilla and orange zest.

Grease a loaf tin and line the bottom with parchment paper. Spoon in the mixture, level off the top and bake for approximately 45 minutes, or until an inserted skewer comes out clean. Cool in the tin for 5 minutes, then turn onto a cooling rack.

To make the plums, place the plums, cut side up, in a buttered ovenproof dish.

Place all the other ingredients in a saucepan, bring to the boil and simmer rapidly until the liquid has reduced by half. Strain through a sieve over the plums, cover with greaseproof paper and bake for 25 minutes at 180°C. Cool and then boil the liquid in a saucepan until it has a syrupy consistency. Pour the liquid over the plums and store in a container until needed – they'll keep in the fridge for up to 2 weeks.

To serve, slice the cake, spoon around some plums and serve with a dollop of cream.

Serve the cake as soon as possible, or store in an airtight container for up to 1 week.

a kitchen year

november

november

By the time November comes around, I relish the dark, cold evenings. Now is the time to hole up, light the fire and cook comforting dishes that will gladden the heart.

Autumn is my favourite season – I love the root vegetables that by now have had the benefit of a frost to intensify their sweetness, slow-cooked stews, evergreen herbs, apple and pear puddings and the excuse to eat creamy pies topped with buttery pastry.

This month's recipes are a veritable feast of all that is good at this time of the year. I've included my favourite stew recipe with wild mushroom pierogis – if you can forage for your own wild mushrooms, so much the better (there are many foraging courses available around the country).

For me, there is nothing as hearty and warming as a big bowl of steaming polenta oozing with fresh Parmesan and here served with home-made Italian sausages. Gnocchi is one of those oxymorons – a light, pillowy yet rib-sticking dish. Mine are stuffed with leeks (at their best now) and baked with a blue cheese and walnut sauce.

In the fish department, leave the grilled sea bass to summer and concentrate now on what we do best – smoked salmon. It's fantastically good for you and it tastes great too!

Apples and pears are freely available now. You could make crumble with the apples and poach the pears, but apple cider cake is a much more interesting and tasty option. As for the pears, roast them instead of poaching and use them to top brioche in a chocolatey ginger pudding like no other.

smoked butternut squash soup

Serves 4

Slightly smoking sweet, creamy butternut squash gives it an intense edge. Roasting the squash naturally caramelises the sugars in the vegetable. These two methods give the finished soup a great depth of flavour.

Crisp sage combined in a pesto with nutty pumpkin seeds (see p. 165) gives some texture to this sophisticated, silky soup.

1 cup woodchips
1 large butternut squash
2 tablespoons olive oil
1 teaspoon chopped fresh rosemary leaves
½ teaspoon salt
4 grinds fresh black pepper
1 medium onion, roughly chopped
100 g celery, roughly chopped
1 Granny Smith apple, peeled, cored and
  roughly chopped
200 g peeled and roughly chopped potato
1 litre chicken or vegetable stock (see p. 11)

Preheat the oven to 200°C.

To smoke the squash, line a roasting tin with foil and sprinkle the woodchips in the middle of the tin. Lay a wire rack on top. Cut the squash through the middle lengthwise and scoop out the seeds. Place the squash halves flesh side down on the rack. Cover the tin with foil and place directly on a cooking ring on your stovetop. Cook for 5 minutes (with the extractor on!). Cool in the tin.

Peel and roughly chop the smoked squash, then toss in 1 tablespoon of the oil, the rosemary and the salt and pepper. Place in a roasting tin and bake until soft and golden, about 30 minutes, tossing occasionally in the pan while cooking.

While the squash is cooking, heat the remaining oil in a large saucepan over a medium heat and add the onion and celery. Cook until soft, then add the apple, potato and stock and simmer for 20 minutes. Add the cooked smoked squash and simmer for 5 minutes. Purée in a blender and pass through a sieve. Check the seasoning and drizzle sage and pumpkin seed pesto (see p. 165) over the soup to serve.

sage and pumpkin seed pesto

Serves 4

This pesto is good with grilled pork, chicken or roasted root vegetables.

2 tablespoons olive oil
handful fresh picked sage leaves
2 tablespoons pumpkin seeds
handful fresh flat leaf parsley leaves
50 g grated Parmesan cheese
2 tablespoons extra virgin olive oil
2 cloves roast garlic (see p. 8)
salt and pepper

Heat the oil in a frying pan until hot. Add the sage leaves and pumpkin seeds and cook until the leaves are crisp and the seeds start to pop, about 30 seconds. Place in a bowl to cool.

Add the other ingredients and blend in a food processor to a smooth purée. Season. This will keep for 1 week in the fridge.

smoked salmon hash with spicy remoulade sauce

Serves 4

Spicy remoulade sauce:
75 g celery
2 scallions, finely chopped
1 teaspoon finely chopped fresh red chilli
2 drops Tabasco
1 tablespoon Dijon mustard
100 ml sour cream
juice of 1 lime
1 tablespoon chopped fresh tarragon leaves
100 g good-quality mayonnaise
salt

Salmon hash:
500 g baking potatoes
1 small red onion, finely chopped
2 scallions, finely chopped
200 g good-quality smoked salmon, sliced into
  thin strips about 3 cm long
handful chopped fresh parsley leaves
salt and pepper

mixed salad leaves, to serve

To make the sauce, peel the outside of the celery with a vegetable peeler. Chop the celery into fine dice, mix in the other ingredients and season to taste with salt. Set aside.

To make the hash, peel the potatoes and cut into 1 cm cubes. Simmer in salted water until just cooked, about 5 minutes. Drain well and cool. Mix the other ingredients together, add to the potatoes and season to taste. Press the mixture firmly into metal moulds.

Heat 2 tablespoons of olive oil and 25 g of butter over a medium heat in a frying pan. When the butter is foaming, add the hash and cook for 3 minutes, then turn and cook for 3 minutes on the other side.

Serve with some salad leaves and the spicy remoulade sauce.

slow-cooked beef ragu

Serves 4

In the late 1980s, I was lucky enough to win a scholarship to a culinary college on the east coast of America. One of the people I met there was a man called Michael DeVito, whose grandmother gave me this recipe for what she called 'gravy'. Theresa was originally from Naples and her gravy was legendary. She slow-braised chuck steak and pork ribs for a day in tomatoes, red wine and loads of garlic. Theresa served this with spaghetti, but I love this with the pierogis on p. 169.

1 litre red wine
handful fresh chopped oregano, thyme and
  rosemary
2 cloves garlic
50 ml olive oil
½ teaspoon ground black pepper
1.5 kg chuck steak, cut into 4 cm cubes
4 tablespoons olive oil
salt and pepper
1 kg pork ribs
2 medium onions, coarsely chopped
75 g celery, coarsely chopped
4 cloves garlic, peeled and finely chopped
1 x 400 g tin chopped tomatoes
450 ml beef stock (make as for the lamb stock
  on p. 57 or use 2 stock cubes)
handful fresh chopped flat leaf parsley

Mix the wine, herbs, garlic, olive oil and black pepper in a bowl and add the beef. Mix well, cover and refrigerate overnight.

Remove the meat from the fridge 1 hour before cooking and drain off the marinade through a fine sieve, reserving the liquid. Pat the meat dry.

Heat 1 tablespoon of the oil in a casserole until smoking hot and add half the beef. Season with salt and pepper. Cook for 2 minutes, then turn over and seal on the other sides. When sealed, remove from the pan and place in a bowl. Add another tablespoon of oil and seal the remaining beef, seasoning it again. Add to the bowl with the other beef and set aside.

Heat the remaining oil in a pot until smoking and add the pork ribs, cooking until golden, about 5 minutes. Remove from the pan and add to the bowl with the sealed beef. Add the last tablespoon of oil and cook the onions, celery and garlic until soft and golden. Return the beef and pork ribs to the pot and add the reserved marinade. Bring to the boil and add the tomatoes and stock. Reduce to a low simmer and cook for 4 hours, occasionally skimming off any fat from the surface.

Remove the ribs from the sauce, pull the meat off the bones while it's still hot and return to the pot. Adjust the seasoning and add the parsley. Serve with pasta or the pierogis on p. 169.

potato and wild mushroom pierogis

Serves 4

In autumn, I love to make a big pot of ragu (p. 168) with these Polish-inspired wild mushroom and potato dumplings. The combination is a perfect antidote to a cold November day. These pierogis would also be great with the Bellingham Blue cheese and walnut sauce on p. 172.

Pierogi dough:

200 g plain flour

½ teaspoon salt

5 turns freshly ground black pepper

1 medium egg

2 tablespoons sour cream

25 g melted butter

1 tablespoon finely chopped chives

1 egg, beaten, for brushing the pierogis

Potato and wild mushroom filling:

400 g potatoes

25 g butter

2 shallots, finely chopped

50 g wild mushrooms, or your favourite regular mushrooms, cleaned with kitchen paper and chopped

salt and pepper

1 tablespoon sour cream

50 g grated fresh Parmesan

To make the dough, sift the flour into a bowl. Mix in the salt and pepper. Whisk the egg, sour cream and butter together and mix with the flour to a dough. Mix in the chives, wrap in cling film and refrigerate.

To make the filling, scrub the potatoes and boil in their jackets in salted water. Peel when cool enough to handle and press through a ricer into a bowl.

Heat the butter in a large frying pan and when foaming, add the shallots. Cook for 1 minute, then add the mushrooms. Stir until golden, then season. Add to the potatoes and mix in the sour cream and Parmesan. Allow to cool.

To make the pierogis, roll the dough on a floured surface to about 4 mm thick – it should be thin. Cut out 7 to 8 cm rings with a pastry cutter. Gather up the remaining dough and roll out again to make more rings. Brush around the edges of each ring with the beaten egg and place a small amount of filling in the middle. Fold over so the edges meet and press with a fork to secure.

Place the pierogis on a lightly floured tray until ready to cook – you can make these up a day in advance and refrigerate until you're ready for them.

When ready to cook, bring a large pot of salted water to boil and add the pierogis. Simmer for 5 minutes, then drain.

To serve, ladle some ragu (p. 168) or Bellingham Blue cheese and walnut sauce (p. 172) on top of the pierogis.

home-made Italian sausage patties with goat's cheese polenta

Serves 4

These are essentially pork patties flavoured with chilli, garlic and fennel seeds. They're slowly sealed off and then braised with red wine, sun-dried tomatoes and onions.

You can buy instant polenta in most supermarkets, and while it's totally acceptable, it's worth sussing out the real McCoy. As a child, I vividly remember visiting the Valvona & Crolla delicatessen in Edinburgh. It was the most unbelievable place I'd ever been in – Parma hams hanging from the ceiling, smelly cheeses and glistening bottles of oil and vinegar. Nowadays, as a special treat and to compensate for the long winter nights, I order a mini hamper from Valvona & Crolla. This will include good olive oil, beans and always polenta. It takes a while to cook, but is like a soft billow of comfort. Sharp goat's cheese is particularly good stirred in at the last minute.

Sausage patties:
1 medium onion, peeled and finely chopped
2 cloves garlic, crushed
1 teaspoon fennel seeds, ground
150 ml red wine
750 g pork mince (preferably organic)
1 dessertspoon chopped fresh oregano leaves
1 tablespoon chopped fresh rosemary
1 teaspoon chopped fresh red chilli
1 teaspoon smoked sweet paprika
1 teaspoon salt

Sauce:
2 tablespoons olive oil
2 medium onions, peeled and finely sliced
2 cloves garlic, crushed
100 ml red wine
200 ml chopped tinned plum tomatoes
200 ml chicken stock (see p. 11)
salt and pepper
handful fresh chopped flat leaf parsley

Polenta with goat's cheese:
750 ml chicken or vegetable stock
225 g polenta
50 g grated Parmesan
75 g goat's cheese
handful fresh chopped flat leaf parsley leaves
salt and pepper

To make the sausage patties, place the onion, garlic, fennel seeds and red wine in a saucepan and boil until all but a tablespoon of liquid remains. Cool.

Mix this with the pork and the remaining ingredients. Form into 8 walnut-sized balls and press down to flatten.

To make the sauce, heat the oil in the pan over a high heat and add the sausage patties. Cook until sealed and golden on both sides, about 2 minutes. Remove from the pan and set aside.

Lower the heat and add the onions and garlic, cooking until they're golden, about 10 minutes. Add the wine and bring to the boil. After 2 minutes, add the tomatoes and stock. Cover the pan with a lid and simmer for 30 minutes. Check the seasoning and add the parsley.

To make the polenta, bring the stock to the boil. Slowly add the polenta in a steady stream into the stock, whisking all the time. When all the polenta is incorporated, lower the heat to a gentle simmer. Cook, stirring frequently, until the polenta comes away from the side of the pan. This will take 40 minutes for traditional polenta and about 5 minutes for the instant variety.

Add the Parmesan and mix well. Crumble the goat's cheese and fold into the polenta with the parsley. Season to taste.

To serve, spoon the polenta into individual bowls, place a sausage patty on top and spoon over the sauce.

stuffed gnocchi with Bellingham Blue cheese and walnut sauce

Serves 4

Borettane onions are sweet and sour-flavoured onions from Italy, They're available in jars (soaked in balsamic vinegar) from good delis and supermarkets. If you can't find Borettane onions, substitute shallots, cooking them whole in boiling water for 10 minutes, or until soft when poked with a knife. Peel when cool enough to handle, then fry in oil for 2 minutes, until golden, adding 1 teaspoon of icing sugar and a splash of balsamic vinegar to finish.

With Cashel Blue cheese well established on the world's cheeseboard, it's nice to see another Irish blue cheese making inroads in the culinary world. Bellingham Blue cheese is made outside Castlebellingham in County Louth and deserves a wider audience. It's soft and creamy and is absolutely gorgeous when melted.

Gnocchi:
2 large baking potatoes
1 tablespoon softened butter
½ teaspoon salt
1 large egg, lightly beaten
1 tablespoon finely chopped fresh chives
225 g '00' strong flour

Filling:
25 g butter
75 g leeks, finely chopped
75 g Borettane onions, finely chopped
salt and pepper
1 dessertspoon chopped fresh rosemary leaves
1 tablespoon mascarpone
50 g finely grated Parmesan

Bellingham Blue cheese and walnut sauce:
25 g butter
1 tablespoon olive oil
1 onion, finely chopped
50 ml Noilly Prat vermouth or dry white wine
100 ml vegetable or chicken stock
250 ml double cream
100 g Bellingham Blue or your favourite blue cheese
50 g chopped walnuts
salt and pepper

To make the gnocchi, bake the potatoes in a 210°C oven for about 1 hour, or until completely soft when pierced with a knife.

When the potatoes are cool enough to handle, but not completely cold, peel them and either press through a potato ricer or mash with a fork. Add the butter and salt and mix well. Add the egg, chives and half the flour. Mix well, then slowly knead in the remaining flour until the dough is firm and not sticky. Wrap in cling film and set aside while you prepare the filling.

To make the filling, heat the butter in a frying pan until foaming. Add the leeks and onions and season with salt and pepper. Cook until soft, about 5 minutes. Add the rosemary and cook for a further 30 seconds. Place in a bowl, cool for 5 minutes, then mix in the mascarpone and Parmesan and check the seasoning.

Bring a large pot of salted water to the boil. Divide the gnocchi dough into 4 equal pieces. Roll each piece into 4 sausage shapes and divide each sausage into 4 pieces. Roll each of these pieces into a ball and press flat with your fingertips. Place a spoonful of the filling in the middle and lightly brush one side with a smear of water. Fold over and seal, crimping the edges shut, then roll into a tube. Repeat with the remaining dough.

Cook the gnocchi in batches. When the gnocchi float to the top of the water, remove from the water with a slotted spoon and drain on kitchen paper. Repeat with the remaining gnocchi.

To make the sauce, heat half the butter and the oil in a saucepan and cook the onion on a medium heat until golden, about 10 minutes. Add the

Noilly Prat or wine and cook until reduced by half. Add the stock and boil until the liquid has reduced by half again. Add the cream and simmer until the sauce has the consistency of single cream. Crumble in the cheese and remove from the heat.

Heat the rest of the butter in a pan. When melted, add the walnuts and cook for 1 minute. Add this to the sauce and season to taste.

Either cook the gnocchi fresh and serve immediately with the sauce, or place the gnocchi in a buttered dish, cover with the sauce, sprinkle over grated Parmesan and bake in a 200°C oven for 15 minutes, or until golden and bubbling. Either way, serve with bread to mop up the sauce.

corn, chilli and scallion muffins with smoked cheese

Serves 4

There's something very soothing about eating warm, golden muffins at this time of year. The best way to enjoy them is served warm, oozing with butter. These are good served with any soup.

200 g self-raising flour
125 g fine cornmeal or polenta
½ teaspoon salt
1 teaspoon baking powder
½ teaspoon baking soda
75 g grated smoked cheddar
1 teaspoon chopped green chilli
½ teaspoon smoked sweet paprika
4 finely chopped scallions
75 g melted butter
1 large egg
175 ml buttermilk

Preheat the oven to 180°C. Line a 12-hole muffin tin with muffin papers or grease lightly.

Sift the flour, cornmeal, salt, baking powder and baking soda into a bowl. Mix in the cheddar, chilli, paprika and scallions.

In a separate bowl, whisk the butter, egg and buttermilk together.

Make a well in the centre of the dry ingredients and mix in the wet ingredients. Don't overwork, but mix well together.

Spoon into the prepared muffin tin and bake for 20 minutes.

creamy beetroot and apple slaw

Serves 4

For this dish, I prefer a rustic red apple, keeping the skin on for extra texture.

400 g beetroot
2 red apples
2 tablespoons red wine vinegar
1 medium red onion, peeled and finely sliced
2 tablespoons good-quality mayonnaise
2 tablespoons sour cream
1 tablespoon chopped fresh chives
salt and freshly ground pepper

Scrub the beetroot clean and boil in salted water until soft. Check by inserting a fork, but it can take 1 hour or more.

Cool the beetroot, then peel. Coarsely grate into a bowl.

Cut the apples in quarters and remove the core. Slice each quarter into about 6 slices and then cut the slices into strips. Toss in the red wine vinegar to prevent discolouring.

Add the apples to the beetroot and mix in the other ingredients. Season to taste.

rachel's apple cider cake with spiced cider butterscotch sauce

Serves 4

Rachel is my young niece and this is one of her favourite cakes (naturally, her number one is chocolate). Surprisingly, this cake goes down well with kids and adults alike. Like the best of cakes, it's better after sitting for a day or two – if you can resist it.

50 g sultanas
100 ml cider
250 g butter, softened
175 g muscovado sugar
75 g caster sugar
4 large eggs
250 g self-raising flour
1 teaspoon mixed spice
1 teaspoon ground cinnamon
2 red eating apples

Spiced cider butterscotch sauce:
reserved cider liquid from soaked sultanas +
   100 ml extra cider
½ cinnamon stick
2 cloves
pinch nutmeg
150 g Demerara sugar
1 tablespoon maple syrup
200 ml double cream

To make the cake, soak the sultanas in the cider overnight.

Preheat the oven to 180°C. Beat the butter and sugars until light and fluffy. Add the eggs, one at a time. Sift the flour and spices into the butter mixture and mix thoroughly. Peel, core and chop the apples and mix into the cake batter. Drain the sultanas, reserving the liquid for the sauce. Mix the sultanas in well.

Butter an 8-inch cake tin and line with non-stick parchment paper. Bake for 45 minutes, or until an inserted skewer comes out clean.

To make the sauce, place the reserved liquid, extra cider, cinnamon, cloves, nutmeg, sugar and maple syrup in a saucepan and bring to the boil. Simmer until the liquid is thick and syrupy, about 15 minutes. Add the cream and boil until the sauce is thick and creamy. Strain the sauce through a fine sieve and serve with the cake.

chocolate and ginger roasted pear pizza

Serves 4

Chocolate pizza might seem a bit odd, but when you find the base is made from rich, buttery brioche dough and topped with creamy chocolate and gingery roasted pears, it starts to make sense. Enjoy this straight out of the oven drizzled with cream – no plates required!

Roasted pears:
2 unripe pears
juice of ½ lemon
30 g cold butter, chopped
25 g caster sugar
2 teaspoons chopped preserved ginger
75 ml Marsala wine

Brioche pizza:
1 batch brioche dough (see p. 56)
20 g good-quality cocoa powder
35 g muscovado sugar
25 g cold butter, chopped
75 g dark chocolate, chopped
50 ml double cream

To prepare the pears, preheat the oven to 180°C.

Peel, quarter and core the pears and toss in the lemon juice. Place the pears in an ovenproof dish. Dot the chopped butter around the pears. Sprinkle over the sugar and ginger. Drizzle over the Marsala and place in the oven. Bake in the oven, basting every 5 minutes, for about 45 minutes, or until the pears are golden and soft. If there's any cooking liquid left in the pan, boil it in a saucepan to a thick syrup and toss in the pears. When cool enough to handle, slice each pear quarter in half.

To make the pizza, preheat the oven to 200°C.

Roll the brioche into a circle ½ cm thick and place on a lightly floured baking sheet. Prick the base all over with a fork.

Mix the cocoa and sugar together and sprinkle all over the base. Dot the chopped butter over the cocoa and sugar mixture. Bake for 10 minutes. Place the pears over the base and sprinkle over the chocolate. Drizzle over the cream and bake for a further 5 minutes.

To serve, cut the pizza into wedges and drizzle with some sour cream or pouring cream.

a kitchen year

december

december

The years spent in soulless restaurant kitchens at festive times always make me appreciate the time now spent enjoying Christmas with family and friends. Now I'm so busy in the run-up to the holidays that the day itself is like a big letting off of steam. Cooking at Christmas shouldn't be stressful – the key is to prepare ahead, have a cocktail around noon and enjoy the whole thing. I'm assuming that if you've bought this book, you must enjoy cooking, so the recipes for December are festive and maybe a bit over the top!

The most common questions I get about cooking at Christmas are for starter recipes different from the norm, something for vegetarians, alternative puddings to Christmas pudding and something to pep up the turkey and ham.

Most people still want turkey at Christmas. I found this out the hard way when I was an extremely enthusiastic student. Keen to show off my new skills to the family, I boned out a turkey, a goose, a duck, a chicken and a squab and stuffed them all into each other. This break from tradition went down like flatulence in the fog! Now I keep the turkey but soak it in brine to keep it moist and baste it with a sugary glaze. I cure the ham in beetroot and top it with smoky shallots, herbs and garlic and oven bake it, basting frequently with wine and honey.

I've included recipes for a cold ham hock terrine with festive accompaniments, olive oil-poached salmon salad and something for the vegetarians – a festive garland that's also good served with the turkey.

As it's Christmas, there are also lots of decadent desserts and a fudge that'll give you the sugar rush to end them all!

festive spiced ham terrine with pomegranate molasses dressing

Serves 10

Ham hocks are cheap as chips but require a bit of labour. They have a brilliant flavour on their own, but the spices in this terrine give the whole thing a really luxurious flavour. All the components in this starter can be made well in advance (up to 2 days), so it's stress free on the big day.

Alternatively, you could make this dish from shredded leftover ham from Christmas Day and substitute 3 tablespoons of pre-made stock for the ham stock.

Serve this with the fig chutney on p. 183.

Ham:
3 ham hocks (weighing roughly 2.5 kg)
1 peeled carrot, cut in half
2 stalks celery, cut in half
1 leek, roughly chopped
1 onion, quartered
a few thyme and rosemary stalks

Terrine:
2 teaspoons coriander seeds
seeds from 6 cardamom pods
1 teaspoon black peppercorns
6 teaspoons whole cloves
1 tablespoon olive oil
3 shallots, peeled and finely chopped
50 g peeled and finely grated ginger root
¼ teaspoon ground cinnamon
1 leaf gelatine
1 tablespoon pomegranate molasses

Pomegranate molasses dressing:
1 shallot, peeled and finely chopped
50 ml port
juice of 1 orange
1 teaspoon honey
1 tablespoon red wine vinegar
4 tablespoons pomegranate molasses
50 ml olive oil
50 ml walnut oil
salt and pepper

To prepare the ham, wash the ham hocks and place in a large saucepan. Cover with cold water and add the vegetables and herbs. Bring to the boil and simmer for about 3 hours, or until the meat starts to come away from the bone when a knife is inserted. Remove from the pan and cool, reserving the stock (which also makes fantastic soup). When cool enough to handle, remove the fat and then start to pull off the meat, removing any rough bits. Place in a bowl.

To make the terrine, toast the coriander seeds, cardamom seeds, peppercorns and cloves in a dry pan for 30 seconds. Grind in a coffee grinder or mortar and pestle. Heat the oil over a medium heat and add the shallots and ginger. Cook until soft and add the ground spices and cinnamon. Cook for 30 seconds. Cool.

Soak the gelatine in cold water for 5 minutes. Heat 3 tablespoons of the ham stock. Squeeze out the water from the gelatine leaf and add to the hot stock, along with the pomegranate molasses. Cool slightly.

Mix the shallot and spice mix into the ham, along with the pomegranate stock.

Lightly oil a terrine mould or loaf tin and line with cling film.

Press the ham mixture tightly into the mould. Gather the cling film over the top. Cut out a piece of cardboard the same size as the top of the mould and press down. Add a few weights or tins and refrigerate for at least 6 hours. Turn out and slice when needed.

To make the dressing, boil the shallot, port and orange juice in a saucepan until the liquid has reduced by half. Blend this with the other ingredients and check seasoning.

To serve, slice the terrine and serve on plates with the fig chutney on the side and the dressing drizzled round.

fig chutney

Serves 8

Fresh figs have always seemed such a decadent fruit to me – pert and dark on the outside, their insides revealing a speckled red flesh. They're good as they are, split and served with some blue cheese and a dribble of honey, or in this case, gently tossed in a hot red wine, sherry vinegar, shallot and honey syrup.

The sultry flavours work well with the spicy ham terrine on p. 182, but this chutney would also be lovely served with some good cheese, smoked or roast duck breasts or with Parma or Serrano ham.

1 shallot, finely minced
1 tablespoon honey
200 ml red wine
1 tablespoon sherry vinegar
6 fresh figs, cut into quarters (or substitute 10 dried figs, soaked in boiling water for 20 minutes, if you can't get fresh)

Place the shallot, honey, wine and vinegar in a saucepan and bring to the boil. Simmer until the liquid is thick and syrupy, about 10 minutes. Remove from the heat and stir in the quartered figs. This will keep in the fridge for up to 1 week.

poached salmon salad with roast baby beetroot and blood orange salad

Serves 8

Poached salmon:
1 teaspoon fennel seeds
1 teaspoon coriander seeds
500 ml olive oil (not extra virgin)
zest of 1 lemon
zest of 1 orange
1 kg salmon (skinned and pin boned), sliced
  into 8
1 teaspoon salt

Roast baby beetroot and blood orange salad:
500 g washed and trimmed baby beetroot
1 tablespoon olive oil
½ teaspoon salt
6 turns freshly ground black pepper
few sprigs thyme
4 blood oranges
1 shallot, finely chopped
1 tablespoon honey
juice of 1 orange
juice of 1 lemon
50 ml extra virgin olive oil
salt and pepper
mixed salad leaves, to garnish

To make the poached salmon, heat a saucepan over a high heat and add the fennel seeds and coriander seeds. Cook until they start to pop, about 30 seconds. Add the oil and turn the heat down. Add the lemon and orange zest (retain the juice for the salad) and simmer for 5 minutes over a low heat. Remove from the heat and allow to infuse for 2 hours. Strain the oil into another pan and warm through on a very low heat.

Season the salmon with the salt and place in a medium-sized pan. Add the infused oil to the salmon, ensuring the fish is covered (do this in batches). Cook for 5 to 10 minutes, or until the salmon is firm to touch but with a little give.

Remove the salmon from the oil and pat dry with kitchen paper (this can be done up to 1 hour in advance).

To make the roast baby beetroot and blood orange salad, preheat the oven to 180°C.

Take a sheet of tin foil and place the beetroots in the middle and drizzle over the olive oil, salt, pepper and thyme. Gather up the foil to make a parcel. Roast for 30 minutes or until soft when prodded with a knife.

Meanwhile, cut the tops off the oranges. Using a serrated knife, peel the skin and pith from the orange. Take a paring knife and cut the segments out by slicing in between the membranes of the orange. Do this over a bowl and squeeze the orange rind when you've cut out all the segments.

When the beetroot is cooked, peel, quarter and add to the oranges.

Place the shallot, honey, orange juice and lemon juice in a saucepan and boil until the liquid is syrupy, about 5 minutes. Mix in the extra virgin oil and season with salt and pepper. Mix into the beetroot and blood orange salad.

To serve, place one piece of salmon on each plate with the beetroot salad on the side. Garnish with salad leaves.

cider brined turkey with maple chilli glaze

Serves 8

1 x 5 kg turkey crown
100 g butter, softened
salt and pepper

Brine solution:
250 g sea salt
500 g Demerara sugar
2 litres cider
2 litres water
2 cinnamon sticks
juice and zest of 2 oranges
1 onion, chopped
handful fresh chopped sage, rosemary and
  thyme

Maple chilli glaze:
1 poblano chilli
1 tablespoon vegetable oil
1 onion, finely chopped
4 tablespoons maple syrup
2 tablespoons cider vinegar
200 ml cider
salt

To make the brine, bring all the brine ingredients to the boil and simmer for 10 minutes. Cool completely and add the turkey. Refrigerate for at least 24 hours. Remove the turkey from brine and pat dry with kitchen paper.

To make the glaze, soak the chilli in boiling water for 20 minutes. When cool enough to handle, remove the seeds and chop roughly.

Heat the oil in a saucepan over a medium heat and add the onion. Cook until the onion is soft and golden, about 10 minutes. Add the syrup, vinegar and cider and simmer until the liquid has reduced by half.

Blend to a smooth purée in a liquidiser and pass through a sieve. Return to the pan and simmer until it has reached a syrupy consistency, **about 10 minutes**. Check seasoning.

To cook the turkey, preheat the oven to 180°C.

Place the turkey on a roasting rack and rub all over with softened butter. Season well with salt and pepper. Cover with tin foil and place in the oven. Cook for 1 hour. Remove foil and brush the glaze all over. Return to the oven and baste every 10 minutes.

A good rule of thumb for cooking turkey is to allow 30 minutes per kilo plus an extra 15 minutes' cooking time. A 5 kg turkey breast will take just over 3 hours to cook and the internal temperature should register at least 70°C. Allow to rest at least 20 minutes before carving.

home-cured porchetta with smoked shallots, garlic and herbs

Serves 8

Porchetta is cured and roasted pork that is then topped here with a smoked shallot, garlic, fennel and rosemary mix. Bathing the whole thing in white wine during cooking ensures juicy, flavoursome pork. It makes an interesting change from the traditional ham.

2 kg pork loin, preferably from a rare breed

Cure:
1 beetroot
1 cinnamon stick
1 star anise
1 tablespoon coriander seeds
6 juniper berries
1 teaspoon cloves
30 g sea salt
100 g caster sugar
6 cloves garlic, finely chopped
2 tablespoons peeled chopped shallots
handful each of fresh chopped sage, rosemary and thyme

Porchetta:
6 shallots, peeled and cut in half
½ cup woodchips (or ½ cup tea leaves, ½ cup Demerara sugar and ½ cup rice, mixed together)
4 cloves garlic
handful fresh chopped rosemary
1 tablespoon fennel seeds
1 tablespoon chopped fresh thyme
100 ml olive oil
1 teaspoon salt
1 teaspoon ground black pepper
750 ml dry white wine

To make the cure, preheat the oven to 120°C.

Line a baking sheet with non-stick parchment paper. Peel and slice the beetroot as thinly as you can and arrange over the paper. Cook for about 1 hour, or until the beetroot is dry and crisp. Cool completely, then grind the beetroot in a coffee grinder until it's a thin powder. Place the beetroot in a bowl and set aside.

Toast the cinnamon stick, anise, coriander seeds, juniper berries and cloves in a dry frying pan for 30 seconds. Cool and then grind to a fine powder in a coffee grinder.

Mix the spices into the beetroot and add the salt and sugar. Add the garlic and herbs. Rub this mixture all over the pork, pressing the cure into the meat. Cover and refrigerate for 1 week.

When ready to cook, wash the pork loin thoroughly and pat dry.

To smoke the shallots, line a roasting tin with tin foil. Sprinkle over the wood chips or the tea mix and place a rack on top. Place the shallot halves on the rack and cover the whole thing tightly with foil. Place directly on a ring and cook for 1 minute. Leave for 5 minutes and remove from the tray.

Blend all the ingredients except the wine in a food processor to a smooth purée.

To make the porchetta, preheat the oven to 200°C.

Score the skin of the pork and rub the shallot purée all over the pork on both sides. Place the pork on a rack on a roasting tin.

Splash a glass of wine over the pork and cook for 30 minutes. Baste with the cooked wine after 10 minutes and then splash on another glass. Turn the oven down to 160°C and repeat the basting until the wine is used up. Cook for 2 hours, basting frequently. Remove from oven.

Place any cooking juices in a pan and boil until they're thick and syrupy. Pour this over the pork, then slice.

vegetarian garland

Serves 8

The great thing about this vegetarian dish is that it not only doubles as an alternative to turkey, but it is also a flavourful accompaniment to Christmas lunch. This garland can be made a day in advance and stored in the fridge.

1 medium-sized celeriac (about 700 g)
1 tablespoon white wine vinegar
1 teaspoon salt
1 tablespoon olive oil
25 g butter
1 tablespoon sherry vinegar
1 dessertspoon honey
1 teaspoon chopped fresh thyme leaves
1 teaspoon chopped fresh rosemary leaves
300 g leek
25 g butter
2 medium red onions, peeled and finely sliced
½ teaspoon salt
6 turns freshly ground black pepper
100 g chopped pecans
200 g of your favourite blue cheese (or use
    sharp cheddar or goat's cheese)
375 g pack of ready rolled puff pastry
2 egg yolks

Peel the celeriac, cut into 2 cm slices and cut each slice into 2 cm cubes. Place in a saucepan with the white wine vinegar and salt. Cover with cold water and bring to the boil. Simmer until the celeriac is just cooked, about 10 minutes. Drain well.

Heat the oil in a large frying pan. Add the celeriac and then dot the 25 g of butter around the pan. Cook for 2 minutes and then stir around. When all the celeriac is golden brown, add the sherry vinegar, honey, thyme and rosemary leaves. Cook until coated, about 2 minutes, and set aside to cool.

Split the leek lengthwise and wash thoroughly, then cut into 1 cm thick slices. Heat the remaining 25 g of butter in a large saucepan over medium heat and add the leek and onions. Add the salt and pepper and cook the leek and onions until soft, about 5 minutes. Check for seasoning. Add the pecans and allow to cool completely.

When cold, mix the celeriac mixture into the leeks and crumble in the blue cheese. Check the whole thing for seasoning.

Preheat the oven to 180°C.

Take the pastry out of its packaging. Lightly flour a surface and roll the pastry so it's about 2 cm wider than its original shape all over. Cut off a 2 cm thick slice and set aside.

Place the pastry so that one long side of the rectangle is facing you with the shorter sides to the left and right. Brush all the edges with egg yolk.

Spoon the celeriac mixture into the middle of the pastry, leaving 2 cm on each side with no filling. Fold over the side edges towards the centre. Brush the edges with egg yolk and then roll into a cylinder.

Place the cylinder in the centre of a lightly floured baking tray. Form the cylinder into a circle, securing the whole thing by brushing with egg yolk where the cylinder meets with egg yolk. Brush the whole garland. Use the strip that you kept at the beginning to make leaves to garnish the garland (you could use a pastry cutter). Brush the leaves with egg yolk. Bake for 30 minutes. Serve immediately.

celeriac and thyme soufflés

Serves 8

300 g peeled celeriac, cut into 2 cm cubes
1 teaspoon white balsamic vinegar
½ teaspoon salt
2 tablespoons olive oil
25 g butter
1 teaspoon fresh chopped thyme leaves
1 small onion, finely chopped
100 g butter
100 g plain flour
300 ml whole milk
4 large eggs
1 dessertspoon chopped fresh thyme leaves
75 g grated Parmesan
salt and pepper
4 tablespoons double cream (optional)
50 g grated sharp cheddar or Gruyère
  (optional)

Preheat the oven to 180°C.

Toss the celeriac in the vinegar and place in a saucepan. Cover with cold water, season with salt and bring to the boil. Simmer until the celeriac is soft, about 10 minutes. Drain well.

Heat 1 tablespoon of olive oil in a frying pan until hot and add the celeriac. Dot the butter around the pan and cook, without moving the celeriac, for 1 minute. Add 1 teaspoon of chopped thyme and stir until the celeriac is golden. Mash with a potato masher and set aside.

Heat the remaining oil in a saucepan over medium heat and cook the onion until golden, about 10 minutes. Add the 50 g of butter and stir until melted. Beat in the flour and then slowly add the milk, beating as you add. Remove from the heat. Separate the eggs and add the yolks to the milk mixture. Whisk the whites in a scrupulously clean bowl to stiff peaks.

Add the celeriac mash, the dessertspoon of thyme and half the Parmesan to the milk mixture and mix well. Fold in the egg whites.

Butter 8 ramekins and sprinkle the remaining Parmesan around the inside of the ramekins. Place the ramekins in a roasting tin and pour in the soufflé mix three-quarters of the way up each ramekin. Pour boiling water into the tray halfway up the ramekins. Bake for 20 minutes. Serve immediately in the ramekins.

Alternatively, up to 2 days before, turn out the soufflés into a buttered ovenproof dish. Refrigerate, and when ready to cook, preheat the oven to 180°C, drizzle the soufflés with the cream, sprinkle over the sharp cheese and bake for 10 minutes, or until golden brown.

panettone with sherry-soaked Agen prunes and orange bread and butter pudding

Serves 8

Panettone is an Italian fruit cake that's become as synonymous with Christmas here as fruit cake or Christmas pudding. It's quite dry, which makes it ideal for bread and butter pudding. Agen prunes are sticky, sweet and sour and lovely. They're a bit dearer than regular prunes, but well worth it. Soaking these Provence favourites in Spanish sweet sherry and baking them with Italian bread in a quivering orange-infused custard made with Irish butter, eggs and cream is a celebration of all that is good in Europe.

75 g Agen prunes
75 g Pedro Ximenez sherry
juice and zest of 2 oranges
1 tablespoon honey
1 vanilla pod
400 ml double cream
4 large eggs
125 g caster sugar
1 shop-bought panettone
50 g butter, at room temperature

Chop the prunes and soak in the sherry for a couple of hours.

Place the orange zest, juice and honey in a large saucepan. Bring to the boil and reduce to a thick syrup – this will take about 5 minutes.

Split the vanilla pod and scrape the seeds into a separate saucepan. Drop in the vanilla pod and add the cream. Heat the cream until scalded, about 2 minutes.

In a separate bowl, whisk the eggs and sugar together until pale and creamy. Remove the vanilla pod from the cream and pour the hot cream mix over the eggs and whisk well.

Preheat the oven to 170°C.

Lightly butter an ovenproof dish. Cut the crust from the panettone and cut into equal-sized slices. Butter the panettone and arrange in the dish, so that the slices are slightly overlapping. Sprinkle over the soaked prunes and pour over the cold custard. Leave for 5 minutes to soak in. Place the dish in a roasting tin and pour hot water halfway up the dish into the tin. Bake for 35 to 40 minutes, or until golden and set, but still wobbly when you shake the dish. Serve immediately.

white chocolate, orange and cranberry fudge

Serves 8

There are two camps of fudge eaters – those who prefer it to be crumbly in texture and those who like it to be creamy and squidgey. I fall into the latter group. This fudge has a real festive feel, makes a great present and is the perfect ending to Christmas lunch.

50 g dried cranberries
25 ml Grand Marnier
juice and zest of 2 oranges
375 g icing sugar
100 ml whole milk
75 g butter
275 g good-quality white chocolate, chopped
2 tablespoons double cream

Place the cranberries, Grand Marnier and orange juice in a saucepan. Bring to the boil and continue to simmer until the liquid has reduced by half, about 5 minutes.

Grease and line an 8-inch baking tin with parchment paper.

Mix the icing sugar and milk in a heavy-based saucepan. Turn the heat down to medium and cook for 1 minute to warm through. Add the butter and, stirring constantly, bring to the boil.

Without stirring, boil the mixture constantly for 5 minutes.

Reduce the heat and add the chocolate and cream. Remove from the heat and stir until the chocolate melts. Stir in the cranberry mixture and orange zest.

Pour the mixture into the prepared baking tray and chill until set. Cut into cubes when cold and store in a plastic container. This fudge will keep for up to 2 weeks.

iced fruit and pistachio dark chocolate nougatine

Serves 8

My friend Chris, who lives in New Zealand now, reminded me of this dessert I used to make. It's a blissful, make-ahead dessert that's perfect as an alternative to Christmas pudding.

100 g assorted dried fruits (cranberries, blueberries and cherries are all good)
100 ml Grand Marnier or brandy
1 tablespoon honey
100 g caster sugar
50 g almonds, roughly chopped
50 g pistachio nuts, roughly chopped
300 g dark chocolate (70% cocoa solids is good)
3 large egg whites
1 tablespoon liquid glucose
100 g caster sugar
100 ml double cream

Soak the dried fruits in the liqueur for at least 4 hours. Place in a saucepan and add the honey. Boil until thick and syrupy. Set aside.

Place the 100 g of caster sugar in a heavy-based pan and cook on a high heat until the sugar melts and is a deep golden amber colour, about 5 minutes. Don't stir the caramel, or it will crystallise. Add the almonds and pistachios, mix well and turn out onto a tray lined with non-stick parchment paper. Allow to cool, and when solid, chop up into small bite-sized pieces.

Lightly brush a loaf tin with oil and line with cling film.

Chop the chocolate and place in a glass or metal bowl over a pot of hot water, ensuring the bottom of the bowl isn't touching the water, as this will cause the chocolate to 'seize'. Allow to melt gently.

Place the egg whites, glucose and 100 g of sugar in a glass or metal bowl and whisk well. Place over a pot of simmering water and whisk constantly until the mixture thickens, becomes voluminous and feels hot to touch, about 10 minutes.

Remove from the heat and gently fold in the melted chocolate, then fold in the cream. Fold in the dried fruits and caramelised nuts. Pour the whole thing into the prepared loaf tin and freeze for at least 6 hours.

Remove the tin from the freezer 10 minutes prior to serving. Turn out onto a board and slice as thickly as you want. You could serve this with cream, but it's quite good on its own.

christmas trifle

Serves 8

Christmas wouldn't be Christmas without a big bowl of trifle. This is a festive variation with spiced orange cake, cherry and orange jelly and cherry custard. Griottine cherries are cherries that have been bottled in brandy. They're also lovely poured over vanilla ice cream. All that's left is to be extremely garish and childish with the decorations!

Orange pound cake:
150 g butter, at room temperature
150 g caster sugar
3 medium eggs
150 g ground almonds
250 g self-raising flour, sieved
1 teaspoon mixed spice
zest of 2 oranges (retain the juice for the jelly)

Cherry and orange jelly:
5 leaves gelatine
juice from oranges above + 200 ml orange
  juice
1 tablespoon caster sugar
250 ml Griottine cherries and their liquor (make
  sure you pack in the cherries)
50 ml Grand Marnier

Sour cherry custard:
100 g dried cherries
1 tablespoon honey
100 ml red wine
500 ml whole milk
1 vanilla pod
5 large egg yolks
50 g caster sugar
25 g cornflour
100 g mascarpone cheese

500 ml whipping cream, to finish
sugar balls, to decorate
toasted almonds, to decorate

To make the pound cake, preheat the oven to 170°C.

Beat the butter and sugar until pale and fluffy. Add the eggs one at a time. Fold in the almonds, flour, mixed spice and orange zest. Pour into a lightly greased loaf tin and bake for 30 minutes, or until an inserted skewer comes out clean. Cool in the tin for 5 minutes, then turn onto a cooling rack to cool.

When cold, cut in half. Wrap one half in cling film or eat straight away. Remove the crust from the other half and cut into 2 cm cubes. Place in the bottom of a glass bowl or individual glasses.

To make the jelly, soak the gelatine in cold water. Boil the orange juice and sugar until the sugar has dissolved.

Squeeze the water from the gelatine and add to the hot liquid. Remove from the heat and allow to cool. Add the Griottine cherries and their liquor and the Grand Marnier. Pour over the pound cake and chill.

To make the custard, boil the cherries, honey and wine to a thick syrup, about 5 minutes.

Place the milk in a saucepan, split the vanilla pod and scrape the seeds into the milk with the pod. Simmer the milk.

Whisk the egg yolks, sugar and cornflour to a smooth paste. Pour over the hot milk and whisk. Return to the pan and stir until thick. Pour into a bowl, remove the vanilla pod, stir in the cherries, cover the surface with cling film and allow to cool completely. When cool, whisk in the mascarpone and pour over the chilled set jelly. Chill for at least 2 hours.

To finish the trifle, whisk the whipping cream to soft peaks (sweeten with 1 tablespoon of icing sugar if desired) and spoon over the top of the trifle. Garnish with gold or silver sugar balls and toasted flaked almonds.

poinsettia cocktail

Serves 8

Starters are sorted and turkey's in the oven? Celebrate with one of these festive cocktails, which makes a refreshing change from a cream sherry.

150 ml orange juice
2 tablespoons caster sugar
50 ml Grand Marnier or Triple Sec
200 ml cranberry juice
750 ml bottle of chilled Prosecco

Place the orange juice and sugar in a saucepan and simmer until the sugar has dissolved. Cool completely.

Pour the orange and sugar solution into a large glass jug. Add the Grand Marnier or Triple Sec and cranberry juice. Chill in the fridge for 1 hour. Mix well. Carefully pour the Prosecco into the jug. Pour into cocktail or champagne glasses.

glossary

'00' flour: Excellent for pasta, breads and cakes. This flour is available in most supermarkets and delis or online from www.valvonacrolla.com.

Black sesame seeds: Available from Asian shops.

Borettane onions: Sweet and sour onions from Italy. Available in jars from Fallon & Byrne in Dublin and most good delis, as well as online from www.valvonacrolla.com.

Chillies: I order chillies online at www.coolchile.co.uk. They stock guajillo, poblano and chipotle chillies as well as cornmeal, tamale wrappers and equipment. Some supermarkets are also now stocking authentic dried chillies.

Dulce de leche: Literally meaning 'sweet of the milk', this liquid toffee is similar to banoffee toffee. Available in most supermarkets and delis.

Gram flour: Flour made with ground chickpeas. Available in most supermarkets, health food shops and Asian or Indian shops.

Limoncello: A Sicilian lemon liqueur. Bring some back from holidays or it's available in good off licences.

Liquid glucose: Available in chemists, health food shops and supermarkets.

Miso: Japanese soy bean paste. Available in many supermarkets or Asian shops.

Orzo: A rice-shaped pasta. Available in supermarkets, Asian shops or delis.

Pedro Ximenez sherry: A lovely, rich, dark sherry that goes perfectly with Christmas pudding and chocolate. Available in good off licences and supermarkets.

Piquillo peppers: Tangy peppers that have been grilled over chestnut wood and packed in cans. Available in Fallon & Byrne in Dublin, good delis and online at www.brindisa.com.

Polenta: Available in most supermarkets in instant form, which takes 5 minutes to cook. Fallon & Byrne in Dublin and Avoca shops stock authentic polenta. For white and yellow corn varieties by mail order, go to www.valvonacrolla.com.

Pomegranate molasses: A sticky, dark concoction made from pomegranates. Its sweet and sour taste makes it good for sweet things (e.g. drizzled over ice cream or for roasting plums) as well as savoury (e.g. in dressings or as a glaze for ham). Available in supermarkets, Asian and Middle Eastern shops.

Quinoa: This Latin American seed puffs up like couscous but is gluten free and slow release. Available in supermarkets and most health food shops.

Salt: I used Maldon salt for all the recipes in this book – crush up the crystals between your fingers before adding.

Smoked paprika: Also known as pimenton, this is available in hot and sweet varieties. I used the sweet variety in the recipes in this book, but feel free to spice things up with the hot kind. Available in supermarkets, delis and online at www.brindisa.com, which is a fantastic site for all Spanish ingredients.

Spices: Most supermarkets now stock previously hard-to-get spices like fenugreek, star anise, nigella seeds and Szechuan peppercorns. Asia Market in Dublin and in Belfast is a good source of spices.

Tahini: A sesame seed paste that's great for dressings and marinades. Available in health food shops, supermarkets and delis.

directory of suppliers

Ballybrado Organic Supply

www.ballybrado.com

Ballybrado Direct sells organic food from 200 certified organic Irish producers so their produce goes directly to the customer.

Bridgestone Food Lover's Guide to Northern Ireland

www.bestofbridgestone.com

The second edition of Caroline Workman and John McKenna's acclaimed *Bridgestone Food Lover's Guide to Northern Ireland* brings you the finest restaurants, describes the funkiest shops and specialist producers, and describes the amazing chefs, bakers, butchers, growers and innkeepers in sparkling prose that brings alive Northern Ireland's unique, creative food culture.

Bridgestone Irish Food Guide

www.bestofbridgestone.com

Described by *The Irish Times* as 'the bible' of Irish food, the eighth edition of John and Sally McKenna's Andre Simon Award-winning directory of the best food and food people in Ireland is recognised as the most essential guide to Ireland's food culture. Here you will find the shops, the restaurants, the producers, the markets and the places to stay. A magnificent mosaic of world-class people and places that neither the resident nor the visitor can afford to be without.

Brindisa

www.brindisa.com

Brindisa imports the most extensive range of high-quality Spanish foods in Britain from the most respected producers in Spain.

Cooks Academy

www.cooksacademy.com

2 Charlemont Terrace, Crofton Road, Dun Laoghaire, Co. Dublin, Ireland

Cooks Academy provides cookery lessons in Dun Laoghaire and their online shop stocks leading brands such as Anolon cookware and bakeware, Wüsthof, Le Creuset, Typhoon, Gaggia, Kenwood and Magimix as well as some of their favourite school gadgets, such as Amco citrus squeezers, microplane graters and Rubbermaid high heat spatulas.

Cool Chile Co.

www.coolchile.co.uk

Mexican dried chillies and other Mexican ingredients to make authentic Mexican food at home.

English Market, Cork

The English Market has entrances on Princes Street, Patrick Street and the Grand Parade in Cork City. It is a covered market for fish, fruit, meat and vegetables, where foods from all over the world as well as traditional Cork foods can be purchased.

Fallon & Byrne

11-17 Exchequer Street, Dublin 2, Ireland

A specialist food shop in Dublin's city centre. Sells a wide selection of fresh fruit and vegetables as well as meat, fish and deli goods. Stocks a large selection of dried goods from all over the world. Modelled on New York-style food halls, such as Dean & de Luca, which sell hard-to-find specialty ingredients as well as reasonably priced everyday products.

Farmers' Markets

www.irelandmarkets.com
www.irishfarmersmarkets.ie

Information and links to farmers' markets across Ireland.

Kitchen Complements

www.kitchencomplements.ie

Chatham House, Chatham Street, Dublin 2, Ireland

Stocks a wide range of cookware and bakeware and delivers worldwide.

Seasoned Pioneers

www.seasonedpioneers.co.uk

Seasoned Pioneers offers an incredibly extensive and innovative range of over 200 authentic spices, chillies, herbs, specialist seasonings and spice blends, including many organic ones.

Sheridan's Cheesemongers

www.sheridanscheesemongers.com

Sheridan's Cheesemongers source quality artisan products and where possible forge links directly with the food producers. Many of their farmhouse cheeses and foods are handmade locally in Ireland. They have shops in Galway, Dublin, Waterford and stalls at farmers' markets around the country.

Valvona & Crolla

www.valvonacrolla.com

Scotland's oldest delicatessen and Italian wine merchant and one of Europe's original specialist food shops, founded in 1934. They list food products and wines from around the world. In the online shop, you will find own-baked bread, cakes and biscuits and an extensive range of cheese, champagne, cookery books, coffee, tea, kitchenware, pasta, rice, salami, sausages, oil, vinegar, port, dessert wine, whisky and wine.

index